# THE ADVENTURES OF
# BARON
# MUNCHAUSEN

## The Screenplay

By Charles McKeown & Terry Gilliam

**APPLAUSE**
**THEATRE BOOK PUBLISHERS**
New York • London

An Applause Original
The Adventures of Baron Munchausen
The Screenplay

Library of Congress Cataloging-in-Publication Data:

Gilliam, Terry.
   The adventures of Baron Munchausen, the screenplay.

   I. McKeown, Charles. II. Adventures of Baron Munchausen
(Motion Picture) III. Baron Munchausen's narrative of his marvelous
travels. IV. Title.

PN1997.1A3114  1989     791.43'72    89-234
ISBN 1-55783-041-X

APPLAUSE THEATRE BOOK PUBLISHERS
211 West 71st Street
New York, NY  10023
Phone 212-595-4735

406 Vale Road
Tonbridge, Kent TN9 1XR
Phone 0732 35775

First Applause printing, 1989.

# THE ADVENTURES OF
# BARON
# MUNCHAUSEN

TITLE
THE ADVENTURES OF BARON MUNCHAUSEN

The title floats in a beautiful sky soaked in late
afternoon light. From the distance, from the bottom of
frame, spread across the screen, appear dozens of
flapping exotic-looking flags. As the credits
continue, they rise in frame, getting closer and
closer. In the center of this procession, the
perfectly circular open mouth of something bronze and
animal-like rises towards us until it fills frame. We
are looking down the mouth of a Turkish cannon. The
credits finish as it comes to a halt. There is a
pause, then the cannon fires and the screen is filled
with smoke and flames.

                                              CUT TO:

A RUBBLE-FILLED STREET where the missile from the
Turkish cannon lands and explodes, blowing up a
passing CITIZEN and sending other CITIZENS running for
cover amidst a shower of burning debris.

                                              CUT TO:

SEVERAL TURKISH CANNON as they continue to fire.
Exotic flags flutter above them.

                    LATE EIGHTEENTH CENTURY
                      THE AGE OF REASON
                         WEDNESDAY


1   EXT.        WALLED CITY AND ENVIRONS        SUNSET

A high panoramic shot of a walled city under siege.
The sun is going down over the horizon, casting a
long-shadowed glow across the blasted landscape. Smoke
pours from the city. Beyond the badly damaged walls
lies the city harbor and the sea where the Turkish
fleet is riding at anchor. The city's fleet has been
sunk in the harbor and the masts of its ships stick
out of the water. In the foreground, backlit by the
setting sun, shimmers the brightly colored Turkish
camp.


2   EXT.        TURKISH CAMP        SUNSET

The Turkish camp full of brightly decorated tents and

                                          (CONTINUED)

pavilions. The cannon ringing the camp are silent. The
TURKISH SOLDIERS are having a feast. Music is being
played, sheep are being roasted on spits, a good time
is being had by all and there is plenty of food. In
the middle of the feast a TURKISH SOLDIER is gnawing
at a bone. Having torn most of the meat off the bone
with his teeth he tosses it carelessly into the air.
THE CAMERA follows the bone as it spins upwards. It
has just about reached its greatest height when it is
caught in the beak of a nasty looking sea gull.

                                            CUT TO:

THE DISTANT WALLED CITY as the sea gull wings away
towards it carrying the bone.

3   **EXT.        INSIDE THE WALLED CITY       SUNSET**

ANGLE ON an EMACIATED MAN in the walled city. He
points a musket into the sky and fires.

                                            CUT TO:

THE NASTY LOOKING SEA GULL as it dodges the ball from
the musket and in so doing drops the bone, which falls
towards the town.

ANGLE ON the ground in front of the EMACIATED MAN as
the bone lands at his feet. He stretches down to pick
it up. As his hand grasps the bone other hands appear
and snatch at it. A struggle follows which turns into
a full-scale fight between a group of EMACIATED
CITIZENS.

Moving away from the fighting EMACIATED CITIZENS we
begin to explore the city within the walls. Tired,
thin, and dirty CITIZENS grub around in the rubble for
food or belongings. Some are tending to the WOUNDED.
As they do so, a horse-drawn hearse rumbles past
stacked with coffins. Many of the buildings in the
town have been flattened and some are on fire. At one
of these fires, a group of FIREMEN are operating a
fire engine and carrying dead and injured CITIZENS
away on stretchers. A group of armed SOLDIERS led by a
mounted CAVALRY OFFICER march past. Some of the
SOLDIERS are carrying a wounded comrade on a
stretcher.

The SOLDIERS move on into the town square where we

                                        (CONTINUED)

3    CONTINUED:

find a huge bronze horse's head lying on the ground. A group of CITIZENS have taken shelter inside it and sit huddled round a fire.

ANGLE ON a huge broken equestrian statue on a plinth. The horse's head has been broken off, and so has that of the rider.

END OPENING CREDITS

The CAMERA sweeps around the statue and down to the plinth on which it stands. There are many official notices plastered on the marble base announcing the latest requisitioning rules, rationings, anti-looting laws, etc. Amongst these is stuck a large poster proclaiming:

THE ADVENTURES OF BARON MUNCHAUSEN

A TALE OF INCREDIBLE TRUTHS

RESURRECTED AND PERFORMED FOR THE FIRST

TIME IN THIRTY YEARS BY THE HENRY SALT

AND SON PLAYERS

Tickets available from the Theatre Royal.

As we are reading the poster, SALLY SALT, a small girl about nine years old, appears from below, scratches "AND SON" from the poster, and replaces it with "AND DAUGHTER." She then looks up at the towering horse and rider with a look of satisfaction. Behind the statue glows a crescent moon. SALLY then turns her attention to another HENRY SALT & SON poster further along the plinth. As she proceeds to make her corrections the CAMERA cranes up and away revealing more of the awful devastation of the town square — fires burn, bodies hang from gibbets; suddenly a great black winged FIGURE looms into frame, floating menacingly over the town. The reverse angle reveals the FIGURE to be a great stone gargoyle hanging from the corner of the ruined cathedral. It is DEATH — black-hooded, spectral, wings spread wide and carrying a scythe and hourglass in his skeletal hands. It almost seems to be watching SALLY in the distance as she continues altering the posters, unaware of its stony presence.

3

## THE
### ADVENTURES OF
# BARON
# MUNCHAUSEN

A tale of incredible *TRUTHS*
RESURRECTED and PERFORMED
for the first time in *thirty years* by

# THE HENRY SALT
# AND DAUG
# PLAYERS.

*Tickets available from* THEATRE ROYAL
BOX OFFICE. *Door 1s. Pit 6d. Gallery 3d.*

---

# PLAYERS. WE

*Tickets available from the* THEATRE ROYAL
BOX OFFICE. *Door 1s. Pit 6d. Gallery 3d.*

**4    INT.        BACKSTAGE        DUSK**

Muffled music of a seafaring kind from a trio of
hidden musicians.

We are in a dark place filled with gears and wheels,
ropes and pulleys. THE CAMERA follows the gears and
ropes to a point behind a braced wooden circular
object which is rising. We stay with this disk until
we emerge above a braced canvas flat and look down
across a stage into the auditorium of a theater. The
auditorium, the roof of which has been blown off, is
full of PEOPLE watching the stage. Many of them have
sustained injuries in the course of the siege and are
heavily bandaged. Others watch the stage from
stretchers. At the back of the auditorium, around
which great broken baroque figures dangle crazily,
some of the boxes have been taken over by the
homeless. These people watch the proceedings below
them while feeding babies, lighting fires, preparing
food, etc. As the music stops, a voice booms out from
the stage and we turn to the AUDIENCE'S P.O.V. to see
that the disk which we followed was a stage sun and
that it is shining over a seascape on which HENRY
SALT, dressed as BARON MUNCHAUSEN, is standing on a
huge cheese island.

SALT
(tongue in cheek)

"And so ... as the sun rose over the
island of cheese, casting long
shadows through the sausage bushes,
illuminating the tops of the honey
trees, and warming the fields of
smoked salmon, I, Baron Munchausen,
who am renowned, first and foremost,
for telling the truth, the whole
truth, and nothing but the truth ... "

Here there are laughs from the AUDIENCE.

CUT TO:

SALT'S P.O.V. to see injured SOLDIERS and CITIZENS in
the auditorium trying hard to have a good time in
spite of the pain of their injuries.

CUT TO:

SALT who glances anxiously towards a box next to the

(CONTINUED)

4

stage as he continues to speak. The box is occupied by a group of official-looking men engrossed in apparently important business.

> SALT (V.O.)
> " ... bade farewell to my three-legged, horn-headed friends, and prepared to return, across the sea of wine, to my native land, there to attempt the education of my provincial, narrow-minded and stupidly incredulous fellow countrymen. For while it has been my privilege to encounter and recognize all that is most wonderful in this world, it would seem that the great bulk of mankind is willfully blind to all but that which promotes boredom, stagnation and dreariness. We heaved anchor and set sail."

                                                    CUT TO:

THE WINGS as SALLY arrives. She sneaks in as if expecting to be grabbed by someone. On a wall behind her is an identical poster to the one we have seen in the square. This poster too has been altered by SALLY, but someone has crossed out the "AND DAUGHTER" and tried to restore the "AND SON." SALLY sneaks past ROSE and VIOLET. ROSE is helping VIOLET with some aspect of costume or makeup.

> VIOLET
> How can you become a great actress like me, poor darling, if you get blown to pieces? Come on.

SALLY pulls back a drape, and peers onto the stage from where we hear Salt droning on. VIOLET, who is clutching a baby, comes up behind SALLY, grabs her and pulls her away from the edge of the stage.

> VIOLET
> (sotto voce)
> Where have you been?

> SALLY
> Eating. Roast beef with potatoes ...
> Plum pudding with cream.

                                            (CONTINUED)

                     VIOLET
                (salivating)
        You little liar! Where?

                     SALLY
        At a banquet. With my friends. On the
        moon.

                     VIOLET
                (lifting her hand
                threateningly)
        Just behave yourself!

                     SALLY
        You're not my dad!

                     VIOLET
        The Right Ordinary Horatio Jackson's
        watching the show tonight, and if he
        doesn't like it he'll throw us to the
        Turks!

The BABY begins to cry, and VIOLET tries to quiet it,
giving SALLY the opportunity to escape.

                                  CUT TO:

SALT in the miniature galleon which is stationary in
the middle of the stage. Clearly something is not
happening which should be happening, and SALT is
getting flustered.

                     SALT
                (emphatically)
      " ... We heaved anchor and set sail!"

SALT glances desperately towards the wings.

                     SALT
                (even more
                emphatically)
      "We heaved anchor and set sail!!"

SALT, panic stricken, glances towards JACKSON. Now
there are a few jeers, shouts and laughs from the
AUDIENCE.

                   AUDIENCE
      Get on with it skipper! ...
                (MORE)

                             (CONTINUED)

4    CONTINUED:

                          SALT (CONT.)
                    He's becalmed!
                    There's been a mutiny! ...
                          (laughs)


5   INT.      **BELOW STAGE      NIGHT**

    BILL, JEREMY, RUPERT and DESMOND and whoever plays the
    Sultan are waiting for their cue.

                          BILL
                          (sotto voce)
                    We should never have come here. I
                    want to go home!

                          DESMOND
                          (scornfully)
                    Home? What's that?

                          BILL
                    Food, safety, comfort.

                          DESMOND
                    You're the victim of a happy
                    childhood, mate.

    SALLY leaps down the steps from the stage.

                          SALLY
                    The waves, the waves!

                          DESMOND
                    Oh, bugger.

    BILL, JEREMY, RUPERT and DESMOND leap into action as
    if electrified, but collide. Eventually they sort
    themselves out and begin working stage machinery
    levers. SALLY also works a lever.

                          RUPERT
                    We're actors! Where the devil are the
                    stage hands?

                          BILL
                    Dead!

                          RUPERT
                    They can't all have been killed.

                                        (CONTINUED)

                              JEREMY
                    Not killed, ducky, suicide. Nothing
                    whatever to do with your acting.


**6   INT.      ON STAGE      NIGHT**

ANGLE ON SALT as the stage begins to undulate in
imitation of waves. The miniature galleon begins to
rock and also to move back and forth across the stage,
accompanied by the sound of wind.

The AUDIENCE cheers.

                                                 CUT TO:


THE WINGS, where we find VIOLET with BABY laboring
over a huge capstan which moves the galleon back and
forth. She is simultaneously operating a wind machine.

                                                 CUT TO:


SALT, on stage.

                              SALT
                         (rocking unsteadily)
                    "But ill luck pursued me. I was blown
                    towards the waiting jaws of a whale
                    of such prodigious length that even
                    with a telescope I could not see the
                    end of him ... "

As SALT raises his telescope a great painted cut-out
whale emerges from the wings. As its hinged jaws open
wide, the boat and SALT disappear behind the cut-out.
The whale continues to be trundled towards the center
of the stage as ROSE and DAISY, dressed as mermaids,
rise from between the undulating waves.

                                                 CUT TO:


JACKSON and his COHORTS in the royal box.

                           FUNCTIONARY
                    Are you enjoying it, sir?

                            JACKSON
                          (puzzled)
                    "Am I enjoying it?" I don't think
                          (MORE)

                                              (CONTINUED)

> JACKSON (CONT.)
> that's a question which falls within
> the parameters of our enquiry, is it?

CUT TO:

ROSE and DAISY on stage.

> ROSE and DAISY
> (singing)
> What will become of the Baron?
> Surely, this time, there is no
> escape!

SALT pops his head out of the whale.

> SALT
> I have learned from experience that a
> modicum of snuff can be most
> efficacious.

SALT takes a pinch of snuff from a box and sprinkles
it around the whale's mouth. He then ducks back inside
as the whale begins to shudder and spout smoke and
confetti from its blow-hole. SALT then rises (on a
telescopic platform badly hidden by the plume)
seemingly supported by the spray.

ANGLE on the auditorium where the AUDIENCE gives a
patchy and lukewarm applause as the curtains close.


7   INT.    THEATER.    BACKSTAGE    CORRIDOR/DRESSING ROOMS

SALT storms into the wings.

> SALT
> (furious)
> Hell's bells and buckets of blood!
> Where were the waves?!!
> The waves?!!

JEREMY, RUPERT, DESMOND and BILL are attempting, too
late, to escape to the back of the theater before
being caught by SALT. Now JEREMY, RUPERT and DESMOND
push BILL forward and hide behind his massive frame.

> SALT
> You incompetent IMBECILE!

(CONTINUED)

                        BILL
          It wasn't me! ... It was her!

BILL points at the sweating DAISY who is slumped,
exhausted, over her capstan.

                        DAISY
          It wasn't me! It was him!
                (to BILL)
          You big pintle!

                        SALT
                (exasperated)
          We're supposed to be professionals!
          And we're trying to stay alive!

Here SALT catches sight of SALLY, as she tries to
sneak away into the back of the theater.

                        SALT
          SALLY!
                (grabbing her)
          Where have you been?!

                        SALLY
          Nowhere!

                        SALT
          Don't lie to me!

                        SALLY
          I'm not ...

SALT marches SALLY along the blitzed remains of
corridors at the back of the theater. They pass ROSE
and DAISY's smashed dressing room.

                        SALT
          Don't you think I've got enough to
          worry about?

                        SALLY
          I was ...

                        SALT
          Yes, I know, playing with dragons!
          Wrestling with angels! ... Wandering
          mindlessly through exploding shells
          and blazing buildings.

                                        (CONTINUED)

Here they pass a room in which DOCTORS are tearing scenery into strips to bind the wounds of injured SOLDIERS and CITIZENS. The SOLDIERS and CITIZENS are eating scenery and props (including wax fruit). SALT leaps in to try and rescue his gear.

> SALT
> (outraged)
> Stop that! Put those down! Don't you dare ... ! This scenery has appeared before every crowned head in Europe! You Philistines! These are props for Anthony and Cleopatra! ...

The CITIZENS, SOLDIERS and DOCTORS drive SALT off.

> SALT
> I shall report you ... Oafs! ... Ignoramuses! ... You don't deserve art! ... You don't deserve theater! ... That's the fruit from Hamlet ... Go on! ... I hope you choke to death.

SALT, temporarily defeated, marches on down the corridor to the door of his dressing room which he unlocks, opens and through which we see his belongings, which include a portrait of the absent MRS. SALT, Sally's mum.

> SALT
> Now ... Stay in here or I shall lock you up!

> SALLY
> Where's my brother?

> SALT
> What? You haven't got a brother.

> SALLY
> (picking up poster)
> Well, you just tell me why it says, "Henry Salt and *Son*"? I'm your daughter.

> SALT
> I should never have taught you to read! ... "And Son" is traditional. That's the way it's supposed to be.

(CONTINUED)

7   CONTINUED:

SALT's attention is attracted by a large theatrical
skip which is moving, apparently of its own volition,
towards a door at the end of the corridor. SALT rushes
to it, blocks its path and flings open the lid. Inside
are BILL, RUPERT, DESMOND and JEREMY. (The skip has no
bottom.) SALT flies into a rage and drags them out.

>                    SALT
>           Get out of there! Get out! You
>           scoundrels! You traitors! Run away in
>           our darkest hour, would you?!

>                    DESMOND
>           Yes.

>                    SALT
>           You weak-kneed, lily-livered ... yes?

>                    JEREMY
>                 (helpfully)
>           Yellow-bellied.

>                    SALT
>           Thank you ... yellow-bellied lot! You
>           give theater a bad name! You give
>           actors a bad name! You give escaping
>           a bad name. Where the blazes did you
>           think you could escape to? Eh?

RUPERT crosses his eyes and points in toutes
directions.

SALT hauls them out and beats them back towards the
stage.

>                    SALT
>           Get back to your dressing rooms and
>           prepare for act II.


8   INT.        THEATER        AUDITORIUM

In the auditorium, the AUDIENCE is milling about
eating crusts of bread, urinating in corners,
discussing each other's wounds and waiting for the
second act. HORATIO JACKSON, in the royal box,
continues to deal with business and receive a stream
of EMISSARIES.

(CONTINUED)

CUT TO:

A CLOSE-UP of the royal box, which is crammed with
FUNCTIONARIES, GENERALS, etc., as SALT appears at the
back hoping to speak to JACKSON. SALT hurriedly tries
to clean the dirt from his costume, that came from the
whale. JACKSON, looking up from a scroll, notices SALT
and beckons him to come forward.

> JACKSON
> (rolling up scroll)
> No ... the Sultan's demands are still
> not sufficiently rational. The only
> lasting peace will be one based upon
> reason and scientific principle.

The EMISSARY takes the document and leaves as SALT
fights his way through the throng to JACKSON at the
front of the box.

> SALT
> (fawning horribly)
> I'm terribly sorry Mr. Jackson ...
> the first act didn't go quite as well
> as we would have liked ... One or two
> little technical ...

> JACKSON
> (pleasantly)
> Please don't apologize, Mr. Salt.
> You're doing your best in difficult
> circumstances.

At this point two SOLDIERS holding a wounded OFFICER
enter at the back of the box. JACKSON sees them.

> JACKSON
> (to SALT)
> Excuse me.

JACKSON nods to the SOLDIERS and takes a sheet of
paper from one of them.

> JACKSON
> (consulting paper)
> AH ... the officer who risked his
> life by single-handedly destroying
> six enemy cannon and rescuing ten of
> our men captured by the Turk.

(CONTINUED)

                        OFFICER
            Yes, sir.

                        JACKSON
            The officer about whom we've heard so
            much.
                        OFFICER
                    (modestly)
            I suppose so, sir.

                        JACKSON
                    (smiling)
            Always taking risks far beyond the
            call of duty.

                        OFFICER
            I only did my best, sir.

                        JACKSON
                    (not unpleasantly)
            Have him executed at one. This sort
            of behavior is demoralizing for the
            ordinary soldiers and citizens who
            are leading normal, simple,
            unexceptional lives. Things are
            difficult enough without these
            emotional people rocking the boat.

The soldiers salute and take the unfortunate OFFICER
away. JACKSON returns to dealing with business as the
terrified SALT retreats, as unobtrusively as possible,
from the box.

                                            CUT TO:


THE AUDITORIUM as the MUSICIANS begin to play some
sort of Eastern music. The AUDIENCE settles into their
seats and falls silent as the curtains open to reveal
the Sultan's Harem. DAISY, ROSE and VIOLET, dressed as
odalisques, are dancing round the stage. As the
curtains open a cut-out cloud, suspended on wires,
begins to descend from the flies. SALT, as BARON
MUNCHAUSEN, stands posed on the cloud. The
"ODALISQUES" look up in amazement.

                        SALT
            "Aaah ... Constantinople ... the
            court of the Grand Turk ... "


                                    (CONTINUED)

                                                    CUT TO:

A SHOT HIGH IN THE WINGS from where dark FIGURES are
lowering SALT. SALT squints down at JACKSON from his
cloud.

                    SALT (CONT.)
          " ... What a surprise that a passing
          zephyr should waft me here ... "

                                                    CUT TO:

THE FRONT OF HOUSE as the cloud reaches stage level.

                    SALT (CONT.)
          " ... Perhaps fate wishes me to teach
          the Sultan a lesson or two."

The AUDIENCE likes this last line. They laugh and
cheer. SALT glances towards JACKSON, whom he sees
staring stony-faced back at him. SALT then steps off
the cloud, which immediately returns to the flies as
the "SULTAN" enters clutching a bottle. He salutes the
"BARON" and joins the "ODALISQUES" who have once more
begun dancing.

                    SALT
          "His Highness, the Sultan, loved a
          good wine, and could never resist a
          wager. Characteristics that were to
          cost him dear ... "

At this point we hear a hoarse, cracked voice
bellowing from the back of the auditorium. The
AUDIENCE turns around to see an OLD MAN with a mangy
DOG tottering down the aisle, towards the stage, with
the aid of sticks. The OLD MAN is dressed in what was
once an expensive, flamboyant, uniform, but which is
now faded and tattered. He looks old and sick.

                    OLD MAN
                  (staggering)
          Lies! ... Lies! ... You scoundrel, I
          won't put up with this! It's intoler-
          able! Stop this travesty! Stop it!

The MUSICIANS and the DANCERS on stage grind to a halt
as the OLD MAN lurches towards them. SALT is
horrified; he is moving his mouth but no sound is
coming out.

                                        (CONTINUED)

                              OLD MAN
                It's an insult, an indignity! I've
                never seen so much rubbish in all my
                life! You don't know what you're
                talking about.

                                                        CUT TO:

JACKSON, in the royal box.

                              JACKSON
                           (puzzled, to
                            functionary)
                Is this supposed to happen?

                              FUNCTIONARY
                Er ... Yes, sir, I should think so.

                                                        CUT TO:

THE STAGE where SALT is trying to get everyone to keep
going.

                              SALT
                "One day, after a sumptuous dinner
                ... The Sultan bade me accompany him
                to his private apartments ... "

At this point the OLD MAN begins to climb, with
difficulty, onto the stage.

                              OLD MAN
                           (feeble but
                            determined)
                This blackguard's an impostor! ... *I*
                am the Baron Munchausen! ... And I
                won't be made a fool of!

                              SALT
                           (frantic)
                Please! ... You cannot come up here!
                We are presenting a performance!

The AUDIENCE now twigs that this is not part of the
program and a general murmur runs around the
auditorium. SALT glances towards JACKSON
apprehensively as the BARON (for it is he) finally
makes it onto the stage.

                                                  (CONTINUED)

                              BARON
                        (struggling to draw
                        his saber)
                  You are presenting mockery! You
                  present me as if I were a ridiculous
                  fiction! ... a joke! I won't have it!

SALT tries to bundle the BARON off the stage. The
BARON's DOG yaps and growls at SALT. The AUDIENCE
laughs and cheers. As the BARON is struggling with
SALT, he manages to draw his saber, and in so doing,
inadvertently slices the tip off the end of SALT's
false nose. The AUDIENCE really loves this. SALT
gestures at DESMOND, RUPERT, JEREMY and BILL.

                              SALT
                  Get him off! For heaven's sake!

DESMOND, JEREMY, BILL and RUPERT look at each other
doubtfully as the BARON begins flaying around,
dangerously, with his saber. DESMOND, JEREMY and
RUPERT try to push BILL forward but instead he
retreats well away from the swirling saber and the
growling DOG. As the BARON lurches about he severs a
rope which sends a giant prop chandelier crashing onto
the stage.

                              SALT
                        (glancing towards
                        JACKSON)
                  Curtains!

The curtains are closed, at which the AUDIENCE boos
and jeers.

                                                CUT TO:

JACKSON in the royal box.

                            JACKSON
                  What the devil's going on?

                                                CUT TO:

ON STAGE where the BARON is lurching around examining
the set and the actresses, apparently oblivious to the
havoc he's created. SALLY looks on, fascinated.

                                              (CONTINUED)

                         SALT
                     (apoplectic)
           Get off! Get off! You cretinous old
           fool! You're ruining the show!

The BARON's DOG keeps SALT at bay.

                         SALT
           Down boy! Down!
                     (almost in tears)
           Somebody get rid of him! ... Get him
           out of here! Quickly! ... Bill!
           Jeremy! Do something! I must talk
           with my audience.

                                                CUT TO:

THE AUDITORIUM as SALT steps through the curtain to
address the excited and fractious AUDIENCE.

                         SALT
           Er ... Ladies and gentlemen ...
                     (darting an anxious
                     look at Jackson)
           I must apologize for this ... this
           most dreadful occurrence. I can
           assure you that we will endeavor to
           continue with the performance as
           advertised in your street.

                                                CUT TO:

ON STAGE where the BARON, who is very weak, is
continuing his investigation of the set and the
ACTRESSES.

                         ROSE
                     (simply)
           Hello.

                         DAISY
                     (inimitably)
           Hello.

                         BARON
           Beautiful ladies, yes.
                     (to VIOLET)
           Beautiful lady.

                                           (CONTINUED)

18

                        VIOLET
          You have really great taste, sir!

                        BARON
          But otherwise it's all quite wrong.

                        DESMOND
                    (Edging towards the
                    BARON)
          Eh, listen, Cocky, we've got a show
          to do.

                        BARON
                    (Apparently taking
                    in DESMOND for the
                    first time)
          Good Lord! Berthold!

                        DESMOND
          Who's Berthold!

The BARON is overjoyed and embraces DESMOND violently.

                        BARON
          How on earth ... ? It's marvelous to
          see you! How are you? Where have you
          been? How are your legs! Where are
          the others?

Looking over DESMOND's shoulder the BARON focuses on
BILL, RUPERT and JEREMY.

                        BARON
          Albrecht! ... Adolphus! Gustavus! I
          can't believe it! ... This is
          miraculous!

BILL, RUPERT and JEREMY look perplexed.

                        BILL
          I'm Bill.

                        JEREMY
          He's Bill.

At this point SALT returns through the curtains.

                        SALT
          Is he still here?! Will you get rid
          of him for goodness' sake!

                                    (CONTINUED)
                        19

JACKSON and a couple of FUNCTIONARIES and GENERALS
walk onto the stage.

> JACKSON
> Is anything the matter?

> SALT
> (desperate)
> I'm dreadfully sorry, sir. We're about
> to begin the second act again. Any
> moment now, sir. If you would just ...

> JACKSON
> (indicating
> Munchausen)
> Who is this?

> SALT
> I've no idea ... Some old lunatic ...

> SALLY
> (stirring it)
> He's Baron Munchausen.

The BARON smiles at SALLY and bows to her. SALLY
returns his smile. SALT, appalled at SALLY's
interjection, signals to her to shut up. JACKSON and
his COHORTS look at SALLY in surprise and then laugh
condescendingly.

> JACKSON
> (humoring SALLY)
> Oh, I see. The *real* Baron Munchausen.

> BARON
> Yes, indeed. And who, sir, may I ask,
> are you?

> JACKSON
> (modestly)
> A public servant. I am responsible
> for, among other things, the
> licensing of this theater.

> SALT
> (for JACKSON's
> benefit)
> This, sir, is the Right Ordinary
> (MORE)

(CONTINUED)

                              SALT (CONT.)
                    Horatio Jackson, who just happens to
                    be winning the war and saving the
                    city.

                              BARON
                    Ha!

                              SALT
                    Now please, leave us.

                              BARON
                    He's an ass! Only I can end this war.

EVERYONE is rather taken aback at this statement.

                              JACKSON
                         (smiles indulgently)
                    Explain yourself.

                              BARON
                    I can end it, because I began it. I
                    am the cause.

The FUNCTIONARIES and GENERALS find this very amusing.

                              JACKSON
                    I'm afraid, sir, you have a rather
                    weak grasp of reality.

                              BARON
                    Your "reality," sir, is lies and
                    balderdash, and I'm delighted to say
                    that I have no grasp of it
                    whatsoever.

SALLY is clearly intrigued by the BARON.

                              JACKSON
                         (stiffly)
                    This man obviously needs a doctor.

                              BARON
                         (alarmed)
                    Doctor?! Doctor?!

                              SALT
                         (anxiously)
                    We will continue with the show. Thank
                    you very much, your Ordinaryness.

                                        (CONTINUED)

                              21

JACKSON and his FUNCTIONARIES exeunt to the royal box.

> SALT
> (to the BARON)
> Right. OFF!

ARGUS barks at SALT and drives him back from the
BARON.

> SALT
> (desperate)
> Please! Please be reasonable. If we
> don't get on with it he will throw us
> to the Turks!

> BARON
> *I* will "get on with it."

To the horror and amazement of SALT and the COMPANY
and before they can do anything about it, the BARON
stomps through the curtains and out onto the
forestage.

CUT TO:

THE AUDITORIUM as the BARON emerges in front of the
curtains. The noisy and impatient AUDIENCE cheers and
jeers him. JACKSON is surprised and angered by the
BARON's appearance.

> BARON
> My lords, ladies, and gentlemen —
> Baron Munchausen, at your service.

The BARON bows. There are a few good humored shouts
from the AUDIENCE which seems to approve of this
version of the BARON.

> AUDIENCE
> Give us another tune on your saber!
> (laughs)

> BARON
> Most of you won't remember me ... or
> my adventures ... but I assure you,
> they are true.

> AUDIENCE
> True, eh? That's the stuff! Tell us
> (MORE)

(CONTINUED)

                              AUDIENCE (CONT.)
                    the truth! Come on, let's have the
                    truth! Quick, before you drop dead!
                              (laughs)

ANGLE ON JACKSON, who instructs a couple of his
GENERALS to silence the BARON. They climb out of the
front of the box and advance across the stage, but the
AUDIENCE disapproves of this and begins shouting that
the BARON be left alone.

                              AUDIENCE
                    Leave him alone! Let him be! We want
                    the Baron! Leave the old geezer
                    alone! Etc.

The GENERALS hesitate and look back at JACKSON who,
seeing mood of the AUDIENCE is against him, recalls
the GENERALS to the box. The AUDIENCE cheer and
applaud at their victory whereupon JACKSON smiles and
waves to them, trying to give the impression that he
accepts the applause as meant for him and his
decision.

                              BARON
                    The truth is, I am the cause of the
                    siege!

The AUDIENCE falls about.

                              WOMAN A.
                    What about the Turks then?!

                              MAN B.
                    You're the cause of the border
                    dispute, are you?

                              MAN C.
                    What border dispute? It's the sea
                    routes we're fighting for!

                              WOMAN B.
                    No it isn't. It's because we refused
                    to pay them tribute money.

                              MAN A.
                    That was last time. It's because they
                    insulted us!

                                            (CONTINUED)

> MAN C.

How?

> MAN A.
>         (thinks)
> I dunno ...

> WOMAN A.
> Their ears are set too close
> together, that's what started it.

> MAN A.
> Eyes! Eyes! How can their ears be set
> too close together unless their heads
> are too narrow?

Members of the AUDIENCE start fighting one another,
and take up the cry of: "Their heads are too narrow!"

> BARON
> You poor deluded fools.

The AUDIENCE calms down, and sheepishly watch the
BARON.

> BARON
> If you will only do me the courtesy
> of accepting the word of a gentleman,
> I will reveal the true cause of the
> war!

The BARON draws and flourishes his saber, which has
the effect of opening the curtains. The COMPANY, who
have all been peering through a tiny gap between the
curtains, are caught unawares and dance off in all
directions, some into the wings and some to take up
positions on stage.

> BARON
> After my return from Egypt, I was
> warmly welcomed by the Grand Turk,
> His Highness the Sultan, who knew of
> my reputation and held me in high
> esteem. In fact, so delighted was he
> with my company, that he offered me
> access to his harem. One day, the
> Sultan brought me a bottle of his
> favorite Tokay ...

**9   SULTAN'S HAREM**

CLOSE ON the SULTAN (played by one of SALT's actors)
as he enters filling two glasses from a bottle. As we
track along with him the set becomes less and less
theatrical. It also becomes far too big for the stage
and develops ceilings and 360° of existence. The
characters lose their theatrical makeup and appear to
be real people ... although all a bit fairy-tale-like.
The SULTAN hands one of the wine glasses to the BARON
(who has miraculously reverted to his younger state).
Lying in a bed of flowers on an oriental rug in front
of the SULTAN is a TIGER. The BARON and SULTAN touch
glasses, and drink. The ODALISQUES look on.

> SULTAN
> What do you think of that, eh?

> BARON
> Not bad.

> SULTAN
> Not bad?! My dear Munchausen, it's
> impossible to find better.

> BARON
> Humbug, Your Majesty! What do you
> wager that I don't procure for you,
> within the hour, a bottle of Tokay
> far superior to this, from the
> Imperial cellar at Vienna, a mere
> thousand odd miles away? Accept my
> challenge ... If I don't succeed you
> may cut my head off. These are my
> stakes. What are yours?

> SULTAN
> I accept. And if you succeed, you may
> take from my treasury as much
> treasure as the strongest man can
> carry.

> BARON
> Agreed. Give me pen and ink and I'll
> write to the Empress immediately.

The SULTAN sends a servant to bring pen and ink.
Meanwhile the BARON leans out of a window at the back
of the stage, and shouts to those below.

(CONTINUED)

                              BARON
            Berthold!


**10  EXT.    A FOUNTAIN SQUARE IN THE GROUNDS OF SULTAN'S
                PALACE.                              DAY.**

The BARON's P.O.V. We see, from above, a group of four
MEN sitting around a table in a square, playing cards.
On hearing the BARON the MEN all look up and
acknowledge him.

                            BERTHOLD
            Coming!

These are ALBRECHT, ADOLPHUS, GUSTAVUS and BERTHOLD,
played by BILL, RUPERT, JEREMY, and DESMOND. (This
scene, like all the scenes in the Sultan's Tale,
retains a highly theatrical style and flavor,
constantly reminding us that we are, in fact, in a
story told by the BARON.)

BERTHOLD gets up from the table and hobbles into the
palace. He has heavy weights attached to his ankles.


**11  THE SULTAN'S HAREM.       DAY.**

The SERVANT arrives with a pen and ink. THE BARON
quickly scribbles a letter. As he is signing it,
BERTHOLD drags his weighted legs through the door.

                            BARON
                      (giving letter to
                      Berthold)
            Take this to Vienna, to the Empress.
            She'll give you a bottle of wine.
            Bring it straight back to me.

                            BERTHOLD
            Right-oh.

Berthold puts the letter into his pocket, unfastens
the weights from his legs, and vanishes like the Road
Runner, whooshing off in a cloud of dust that digs a
hole in the floor, then takes him out of the door at
incredible speed. The BARON, followed by the Sultan,
leaps across to the window and looks out.

**12 EXT.    VIEW FROM THE HAREM WINDOW    DAY**

The BARON and SULTAN'S P.O.V. as they look out of the
window just in time to see BERTHOLD appear outside the
city walls and zoom away over the horizon, leaving a
thin trail of dust.

**13 INT.    THE SULTAN'S HAREM    DAY**

The BARON and SULTAN withdraw from the window. The
SULTAN dramatically sets up an hourglass. The BARON
produces his own mini hour-glass from his waistcoat
pocket and sets it going simultaneously with the
SULTAN's. He then returns it to his pocket. The BARON
and SULTAN drink a toast.

> SULTAN
> Perhaps you would care for a little
> light entertainment while you wait. I
> have been composing a short Opera;
> would you like to hear a song or two?

> BARON
> No, thank you.

> SULTAN
> Oh, you'll love it. It's a Comedy.
> It's called The Torturer's
> Apprentice. Here's the Overture.

The SULTAN seats himself at the Torturetron and begins
to play. The MUSIC is accompanied by groans and
shrieks from inside the strange keyboard instrument.
From time to time a SHAKY HAND pushes up the lid of
the Torturetron from within and a "CHORISTER" tries to
escape. He is beaten back by a guard.

> SULTAN
> (spoken)
> Now, the curtain rises on a typical
> everyday Torture Chamber. Yosrick the
> young apprentice sings of his joy in
> his job.
> (sings)
> A Torturer's Apprentice went his
> merry way to work one day.
> I bend and stretch and ply my trade
> Making people all afraid
> (MORE)

(CONTINUED)

                         SULTAN (CONT.)
               But things look black
               Business is slack
               There's no one on the rack but me.
                    (spoken)
               There's something of a recession in
               his business you see, owing to the
               spread of various nauseating liberal
               sentiments. In fact, he has only one
               victim that day — a beautiful 17 year
               old girl whom he recognizes in a rack
               song as his old playmate Griselda.

GRISELDA'S voice comes out of the Torturetron, and is
Operatic screaming, sung in perfect pitch but in great
pain.

                         GRISELDA
                    (sings)
               Ah. Ah. Ah ... Ah . . Ah. Ah
               Oh. Oh O . . oo . . Oh.
               Ah. Ah. Ah. Ah. Ah  ...

                         SULTAN
          Is it you?

                         GRISELDA
          It is me!

                         SULTAN
          Is it you?

                         GRISELDA
          It is me!

                         SULTAN
          You You You!

                         GRISELDA
          Me! Me! Me!

                         SULTAN
          Oh horror! Torn between his love, his
          job and her fingernails.

FADE TO time passing with the sand in the hour-glass.
FADE BACK up on the SULTAN. He is still going strong
at the Opera. The BARON is cross-eyed with boredom and
distaste. The SULTAN, while continuing with the
dialogue and song below, looks at the near empty

                                        (CONTINUED)

hour-glass, smiles at the BARON and beckons forwards
his EXECUTIONER. The EXECUTIONER is a fat, sweaty man
with a large shiny scimitar. He is blind. His small
assistant always leads him around. Together, they
begin measuring and preparing the BARON's neck by
drawing a dotted line around it. The BARON checks his
personal hour-glass and glances at BERTHOLD's weights.

> SULTAN
> (beckoning the
> EXECUTIONER)
> Act Four is set in an Abbatoir. I see
> a lot of slapstick. We begin with the
> arrival of the Eunuch's Chorus who
> sing "Cut off in my prime, mein
> hertz, mein hertz."
>> (sings in a rich
>> falsetto)
> Cut off in my prime
> Surrounded by beautiful women all the
> time
> A Eunuch's life is hard
> A Eunuch's life is hard
> A Eunuch's life is hard
> And nothing else.

> BARON
> (rising)
> Excuse me a moment.

> SULTAN
> Oh, you won't want to miss this aria
> ... it reminds me of my school days
> in England.

He launches into it.

> SULTAN
> (sings)
> Life is rather like a game
> It's important that you win
> And though it is a terrible shame
> If you lie and cheat and sin
> Play up and WIN the game.

The BARON whistles sharply.

(CONTINUED)

> SULTAN
> (sings)
> And never count the cost
> It matters not how you played the
> frame
> As long as you haven't lost.

The BARON whistles again. Seconds later BUCEPHALUS gallops into the harem, scattering GUARDS, SERVANTS, and ODALISQUES.

> BARON
> (leaping onto
> Bucephalus)
> Back in five minutes.

The BARON on BUCEPHALUS jumps out of the window.


14  EXT.    SULTAN'S PALACE    DAY

The BARON, astride BUCEPHALUS, leaps from the very high window into the yard.


15  EXT.  A SQUARE IN THE GROUNDS OF THE SULTAN'S PALACE
DAY

The BARON on BUCEPHALUS lands nearby and gallops up to his EXTRAORDINARY SERVANTS who are sitting around a table playing cards. Throughout the following we continue to hear the SULTAN singing in his harem above.

> BARON
> (breathless)
> Where the hell's Berthold?!

> GUSTAVUS
> Dunno.

> ALBRECHT
> I thought he was with you.

> BARON
> If he's not here in three and a half
> minutes, the Sultan's going to cut
> off my head!

(CONTINUED)

                         ADOLPHUS
                          (pause)
            And?


                           BARON
              "And"?


                         ADOLPHUS
            Is that all? ... I'm sorry ... I
            don't find that funny.
                          (turning to the
                          others)
            Do you find that funny?


                           BARON
            This isn't a joke! ... It's a wager!


                            ALL
                          (leaping to their
                          feet)
              A wager!

GUSTAVUS jumps up, drops down onto his knees, and
presses one of his large ears to the ground.

                         GUSTAVUS
            He's asleep! I can hear him snoring!
            ... About nine hundred miles away.


                         ALBRECHT
              Come on!

ADOLPHUS hops onto ALBRECHT's outstretched hands and
is catapulted onto a parapet and peers out over the
landscape.

                         ADOLPHUS
            He's under a tree! Near Belgrade.
            There's a bottle beside him.


                         ALBRECHT
                          (throwing a huge
                          musket to Adolphus)
            I hope he hasn't been at it.

ADOLPHUS raises the musket to his shoulder.

                         ADOLPHUS
                          (adjusting sights)
            What's the wind speed, Gus?

(CONTINUED)

> GUSTAVUS
> (wiggling ears)
> Three knots.

ADOLPHUS takes aim, and fires it with a great
explosion and bolt of flame.

## 16 EXT.      UNDER A TREE OUTSIDE BELGRADE      DAY

ANGLE ON BERTHOLD lying asleep under a tree on the
outskirts of Belgrade. The bottle of Tokay is by his
side. Suddenly something ricochets off the tree above
his head, shaking it, and causing bits of branch,
twigs, leaves and acorns to fall on top of him.
BERTHOLD wakes up, realizes that he's late, and tears
off without the bottle, returning to get it two
seconds later.

## 17 EXT.    SULTAN'S HAREM

ANGLE ON the hour-glass which is now almost empty. The
EXECUTIONER'S ASSISTANT is preparing the chopping
block which stands in the center of the harem. A
moment later the BARON rushes in, glances at the
hour-glass and looks to the horizon.

CUT TO:

BARON'S P.O.V.— there is no sign of BERTHOLD on the
horizon — nothing. Throughout the above action the
SULTAN sings the following:

> SULTAN
> (sings)
> If I have enemies who hate my guts
> I've no judge and court to try them
> I pop them into boiling oil
> And then I quickly fry them.
>
> If they forgive me, singing hymns
> I try pulling off their limbs
> How quickly they abandon when
> They haven't got a leg to stand on
> then.
>
> I'm a modern man
> These days I find
> (MORE)

(CONTINUED)

                         SULTAN (CONT.)
            You have to be awfully cruel to be
            kind.

            I'm a modern man
            You will agree
            It's either you or me.

The SULTAN peers at the hour-glass with his weak eyes.
There are only a few grains of sand left in it.

                         SULTAN
                    (stopping singing)
            Well, time's nearly up, I think.

The SULTAN raises his hand. The EXECUTIONER'S
ASSISTANT helps the BARON to kneel with his head on
the chopping block. The EXECUTIONER takes his position
and lifts his sword. The SULTAN has his eye on the
hour-glass. Does the BARON hear something? He twists
his head to look to the horizon.

                                            CUT TO:

THE BARON'S P.O.V. as BERTHOLD appears in the distance
and etches his way across the landscape at amazing
speed.

ANGLE ON the BARON as he starts to speak and the
SULTAN's arm drops. The EXECUTIONER's sword swishes
downwards and BERTHOLD zooms into the terrace. The
blade stops just as it touches the back of the BARON's
neck. BERTHOLD skids to a halt, plowing deep into the
floor of the terrace, concertina-ing the marble paving.

The BARON looks at the hourglass and whips out his
personal mini-hour-glass to check as a final grain
falls.

BERTHOLD, lying in the trough, hands out the bottle of
Tokay and a letter for the BARON.

                         BERTHOLD
            I'm not late, am I?

                         BARON
                    (weak at the knees)
            No, no ... not late ... Thank you
            very much.

                                        (CONTINUED)
                         33

As he stands a plait of his hair falls to the ground —
he glances at it:

> BARON
> I needed a trim.

The SULTAN is delighted as he greedily samples the
bottle of Tokay.

> SULTAN
> Hmmm. Delicious. You win.

The SULTAN claps his hands and the TREASURER steps
forward and bows.

> SULTAN
> Treasurer, allow my friend here to
> take from the treasury as much as the
> strongest man can carry.

18  INT.    **THE SULTAN'S TREASURY**    DAY

The entrance, where the TREASURER unlocks a heavy iron
door and admits the BARON, ALBRECHT, ADOLPHUS,
GUSTAVUS and BERTHOLD to a chamber full of gold bars,
coins, chests full of precious stones, etc.

DISSOLVE TO:

19  INT.    **THE SULTAN'S TREASURY**    LATER

ALBRECHT, loaded with treasure from the now empty
chamber, is being guided out of the door by the BARON
and the rest of the GANG. The TREASURER is extremely
worried. He watches the BARON and CO. with disapproval
before hurrying purposefully away.

20  INT.    **THE SULTAN'S BATHS**    DAY

The SULTAN, sitting on cushions and surrounded by the
ODALISQUES, is drinking his Tokay. The SULTAN'S TIGER
is with him as usual. The TREASURER enters and bows
low. He is terrified. He explains to the SULTAN what
has just happened in the treasury. The SULTAN leaps up
in a rage, snatches a scimitar from one of the GUARDS,
and cuts off the TREASURER'S head with one blow. He
then runs from the chamber followed by the GUARDS. One
of the ODALISQUES is left holding the TREASURER's head

(CONTINUED)

which fell into her lap. She is horrified. The
TREASURER's head winks at her.

## 21 EXT.     FOUNTAIN SQUARE     DAY

The BARON and CO. guide the heavily laden ALBRECHT.
Suddenly, the furious SULTAN appears above them with a
couple of dozen GUARDS. The SULTAN gives an order and
the GUARDS advance on the BARON and CO. In response to
this, GUSTAVUS steps forward, takes a deep breath, and
blows the GUARDS and the SULTAN back up the steps. As
he does this, another group of GUARDS appears below
them, and GUSTAVUS turns around and gives this group
the same treatment. By this time the SULTAN and the
GUARDS above have recovered and begin to advance
again, as do the GUARDS below. The BARON draws his
saber and GUSTAVUS takes another deep breath. It looks
as if they may be in for a tough fight. The SULTAN now
shouts another order, and the wall next to the BARON
is shattered as a huge cannon-ball crashes into it.
Looking up, the BARON and CO. see the parapet
surrounding the stairwell is bristling with cannon
barrels. As these cannon fire, the walls surrounding
the BARON and CO. collapse, and are seen to be the
walls of the stage set which is collapsing around the
BARON and ACTORS as the real cannon-balls of the
besieging Turks crash into the town and theater.

## 22 INT.     ON STAGE     NIGHT

As the real bombardment begins, the BARON (old again)
steps forward and addresses the AUDIENCE and JACKSON.

> BARON
> And so ... as you can see, the Sultan
> is still after my head.

The AUDIENCE rises from their seats, on the verge of
panic, as debris falls throughout the collapsing
theater.

> BARON
> Wait! stop! Don't go! Don't leave! I
> haven't finished. There's more,
> there's more!

For a second the AUDIENCE hesitates, still under the
BARON's spell. The BARON's shadow, thrown by a

(CONTINUED)

guttering footlight, fills the stage and seems to stretch out to embrace the AUDIENCE.

The BARON appeals to JEREMY, BILL, DESMOND and RUPERT, who are standing in the middle of the stage.

>                    BARON
>          Gustavus, Adolphus, Albrecht! We're
>          about to make off with the Sultan's
>          treasure. We can't just stop.
>          Berthold?!

>                    DESMOND
>          The name's Desmond, mate. We're
>          actors, not figments of your
>          imagination. Get a grip.

Another shell lands close by, breaking the spell and sending the AUDIENCE screaming for the exit. The BARON appears to crumple slightly as if his energy has left him.

>                    BARON
>                  (feebly)
>          Come back! ... Come back!  ...

                                             CUT TO:

JACKSON AND CO. in the royal box where they are all getting in each other's way as they attempt to escape. JACKSON struggles out onto the stage.

>                    JACKSON
>          What the devil is the  Sultan playing
>          at? It's Wednesday, isn't it?

SALT limps across the stage to JACKSON.

>                    SALT
>                  (abject)
>          I'm terribly sorry, sir, about the
>          show. One or two minor setbacks here,
>          sir.

>                    JACKSON
>                  (objectively)
>          This theater is closed. I want you
>          and your company out of this city by
>          tomorrow.

                                        (CONTINUED)

                          SALT
          Oh, no, sir, no ... Oh sir, sir, sir,
          please!
                    (pulling broadsheets
                    from his pocket as
                    he chases after him)
          Look at these favorable endorsements
          from all over Europe, sir.
                    (reading)
          "Henry Salt and Son holds a mirror up
          to nature.": Vienna Clarion. "Great
          value for money.": Paris Echo. "A
          good night out.": Glasgow Herald.
          Just give us one second.

JACKSON and his entourage hurry away, crossing the
stage and knocking the BARON aside as they go. SALT
chases after them, pleading, as more shells land in
and around the theater bringing down part of the
proscenium arch, filling the place with smoke and
dust.

                                              CUT TO:

SALLY, who is sheltering backstage under a props
table. As the dust begins to clear the BARON's DOG
finds SALLY, whimpers agitatedly, and makes all the
signs indicating that it wants SALLY to follow it.
SALLY does so, crawling through the rubble and dust.
At the back of the stage, in a tent of collapsed
rubble and masonry, SALLY sees the recumbent figure of
the BARON, on whose chest is kneeling the hooded,
black-winged, skeletal figure of DEATH. Propped beside
DEATH is his scythe and hourglass. The hourglass
contains a tiny amount of sand still to run out from
the upper chamber.

DEATH has one hand on the BARON's neck while with the
other he is struggling to pull a fluttering, glowing
something from the BARON's mouth. DEATH seems to sense
SALLY's presence and turns to see her. Surprised and
angered by this interruption, DEATH rears up, wings
spread wide and hood falling back to reveal a shock of
red hair flapping scraggily from a rotten skull. He
looks monumental and horrible. SALLY is terrified.
DEATH advances towards her. SALLY picks up a
candelabra and makes as if to throw it at DEATH who
shudders and transmogrifies into harmless items of
props and bits of theatrical costume lying around the
stage. The BARON's DOG stops growling and moves to the

                                       (CONTINUED)

BARON wagging its tail. SALLY steps towards the BARON.
As she does so she instinctively turns the hourglass
upside down, preventing the final grains from running
out. At this moment the BARON stirs and opens his
eyes. From his recumbent position on the floor, Sally
is framed with a pair of theatrical prop wings hanging
from the theater roof ... and she seems to take on the
appearance of an angel, as she holds a candelabra up
to peer more closely at him.

>                    SALLY
>           Are you all right?

>                    BARON
>                 (feebly)
>           Am I dead?

>                    SALLY
>           No.

>                    BARON
>           Blast!

>                    SALLY
>                 (pauses)
>           Who are you *really*?

>                    BARON
>                 (groans with
>                 disgust)

>                    SALLY
>           Baron Munchausen isn't real. He's
>           only in stories.

>                    BARON
>                 (exasperated)
>           Go away ... I'm trying to die.

>                    SALLY
>                 (puzzled)
>           Why?

>                    BARON
>           Because ... I am tired of the world
>           ... and the world is evidently tired
>           of me.

>                    SALLY
>           But why?

(CONTINUED)

SALLY prods him.

> SALLY
> (repeats)

Why?

> BARON
> (goaded by Sally's
> persistence)

Why? Why? Why? ... Because it's all
logic and reason now ... Science ...
Progress ... The laws of hydraulics
... The laws of social dynamics, the
laws of this, that and the other ...
No place for three-legged cyclopes
from the South seas ... No place for
cucumber trees ... or oceans of wine
... No place for me ...

> SALLY

What happened in the story?

> BARON

What?

> SALLY

In the Sultan's palace ... Did you
escape? ... Were you killed?

> BARON
> (very tired)

I don't know ... It was all a long
time ago ... Who cares?

> SALLY

I do.

> BARON

I'm very tired. Good-bye.

> SALLY

Please tell me.

> BARON

No.

> SALLY

Go on.

(CONTINUED)

> BARON
>> Buzz off!

>> SALLY
>>> (suddenly cross and
>>> impatient)
>> Tell me!

The BARON is rather surprised by SALLY's vehemence.

>> SALLY
>>> (pause)
>> Please.

The BARON begins to believe that SALLY might just have
the makings of a loyal and responsive audience. In
fact he's almost hooked on the idea.

>> BARON
>> You really want to know, don't you?

Another shell crashes into the theater, knocking down
more of the wall. SALLY freaks out and bursts into
angry tears.

>> SALLY
>> Stop it! ... Stop it! ... We'll all
>> be killed! ... And then I'll *never*
>> know the end of the story!

Another cannonball smashes into the back of the
theater. SALLY is furious. She runs out onto the
stage, jumps into the auditorium, and races off over
the demolished wall into the smoke-filled square.

>> BARON
>>> (shouting after her)
>> Wait! Wait, where are you going?!

> CUT TO:

THE BARON's P.O.V. of SALLY as she disappears into the
town square.

ANGLE ON the BARON.

>> BARON
>> Come back! ... Take cover!  ...

The BARON drags himself out from under his scenery

(CONTINUED)

shelter, hobbles across the stage, and stomps off,
with difficulty, in pursuit of SALLY. The DOG trots
beside him.

> BARON
> Wretched child!

23  EXT.      **THE MAIN SQUARE**      **NIGHT**

ANGLE ON SALLY as she runs through the main square.
Buildings are burning around her, and CITIZENS are
running for cover. She passes the gibbet to which the
body of the HEROIC OFFICER has now been added. SALLY
runs into the cathedral.

24  INT.      **CATHEDRAL**      **NIGHT**

SALLY runs through the cathedral which has been
converted into a hospital. All around are DEAD and
DYING. A group of DOCTORS is amputating a SOLDIER's
leg. SALLY hurries through and out of the building.

25  EXT.      **THE TOP OF THE CITY BATTLEMENTS**      **NIGHT**

ANGLE ON a GUN CREW who are sitting beside their
cannon on the battlements, discussing the situation.
Turkish shells and cannon-balls are hurtling past
them.

SALLY runs up the steps to the battlements, a few
yards away from the gunners. She jumps on top of the
crenelated outer wall and begins angrily throwing
stones into the swirling dust and smoke beyond.

> SALLY
> (shouting)
> Stop it! Stop it!

> GUNNER A
> Shouldn't we be firing back at them,
> Sir?

> COMMANDER
> No firing on Wednesdays, it's in the
> rules.

(CONTINUED)

41

                         GUNNER A
          I know, Sir, but ...

                         COMMANDER
          If we fire back at them, that's
          tantamount to saying that either we
          *don't* know it's Wednesday and are
          thoroughly confused, or we *do* know
          it's Wednesday but don't care.

                         GUNNER A
          But why are they doing it, Sir?

                         GUNNER B
          Maybe they want us to think it's
          Tuesday or Thursday.

                         COMMANDER
          In my view, they're trying to
          undermine our values — everything we
          stand for. Wednesday has been
          half-day closing in this town since
          1592. It's our tradition. "Half-day
          closing — all day Wednesday." If we
          let that go, it's the beginning of
          the end.

The BARON followed by ARGUS staggers up to SALLY as a
cannonball strikes the wall a few yards away,
showering them both with dust and lumps of stone.

                         BARON
          Get down!

SALLY picks up a piece of stone and hurls it towards
the enemy.

                         SALLY
          No!

                         BARON
          You'll get us both killed!

                         SALLY
                    (throwing another
                    rock)
          I thought you wanted to die!

(CONTINUED)

>              BARON
>          (out of breath)
>      Yes, but I'm old enough.

Another enemy cannonball thumps into the wall nearby,
throwing out more fragments of stone. The BARON walks
a few yards along the wall to the GUN CREW who are
sitting idly by their cannon.

>              BARON
>          (to the gun crew)
>      Gentlemen, wouldn't it be a good
>      thing, if you were to silence that
>      enemy cannon?

The GUN CREW all shake their heads.

>              COMMANDER
>      No, Sir.

>              BARON
>      No?

>              COMMANDER
>          (incredulous)
>      It's Wednesday!

The BARON is unable to believe his ears. He exchanges
a look with SALLY, who clearly also thinks that this
sounds stupid. At this point another cannonball hits
the wall close by. The BARON snatches up a mortar
shell and drops it onto the barrel of the mortar, thus
firing the mortar. He then grabs the shell as it
emerges and shoots off with it towards the Turkish
camp. The BARON disappears out into the smoke on the
mortar shell, leaving SALLY and the GUN CREW
open-mouthed.


26  **EXT.    WITH THE BARON, ON THE MORTAR SHELL    NIGHT**

The BARON, clutching the mortar shell, soars through
the air high above the turkish camp. The fuse of the
mortar smolders in front of him. He tries to blow it
out.


27  **EXT.    THE BARON'S P.O.V. FROM ABOVE THE TURKS    NIGHT**

We see, below us, through the murk, groups of Turkish

(CONTINUED)

SOLDIERS advancing stealthily towards the city with
ladders, towers, battering rams and elephants with
battle towers on their backs. Suddenly the view
revolves and we are looking up towards the stars.

**28 EXT.      THE BARON ON MORTAR SHELL      NIGHT**

The BARON is hanging upside down from the mortar
shell, desperately trying to right himself.

**29 EXT.      A TURKISH CANNON ON THE GROUND      NIGHT**

Behind the Turkish lines, a group of TURKISH GUNNERS
fire their cannon.

**30 EXT.        WITH THE BARON ON THE MORTAR SHELL AND
                CANNONBALL                      NIGHT**

ANGLE ON the BARON where we see, from behind his
shoulder, the flash of the Turkish cannon below, and
the Turkish cannonball zooming up towards him. The
BARON shifts the path of his outward bound mortar
shell, grabs the Turkish cannonball as it passes him,
and begins his journey back towards the town. He looks
back to see his shell hit the Turkish cannon blowing
it to smithereens. He smiles.

Continuing on his way he overtakes the spectral,
hooded figure of DEATH. DEATH, irritated at being
overtaken, swings at the BARON with his scythe. The
BARON ducks and accelerates exultantly on.

**31 EXT.      ON THE TOWN BATTLEMENTS      NIGHT**

SALLY and the GUN CREW and ARGUS are peering out into
the smoke and murk when they see the BARON zooming
towards them. The GUNNERS duck down behind the
crenelated wall as the BARON lets go of his cannonball
(which continues into the town), spreads his coat to
make a parachute, and glides down to land fairly
roughly beside them. The BARON now looks marginally
younger than he did at the beginning of the evening,
but on landing he twists his ankle, ricks his back,
sprains his wrist, etc. (i.e., he isn't Superman).

(CONTINUED)

> BARON
> Ow! ... Ah! ... Oh! ... The Turks are
> about to storm the walls!

> SALLY
> (awed)
> You really are Baron Munchausen.

The GUNNERS can't believe what they've seen but, at
that moment, the cannon takes a direct hit, and the
entire GUN CREW are killed.

> SALLY
> (grabbing the BARON)
> Come on!

SALLY hustles the BARON down the steps, off the
battlements.

32 **EXT.**     **STREET IN FRONT OF THEATER**     **NIGHT**

The city is burning again, and shells and cannonballs are
raining down. A loose horse bolts past dragging an empty
carriage, with one wheel broken off. The coachman's
boots are still on the driving platform. As it hurtles
past the theater, a distraught SALT appears in the
doorway. The other members of the company are with him.

> SALT
> (beside himself)
> That's it, it's the end, it's all
> over! Generations of theatrical
> expertise snuffed out in the
> twinkling of an eye!

SALLY appears dragging the limp BARON across the
square. ARGUS sticks close to the BARON.

> SALT
> Sally! ...
> (pulling her away
> from the BARON)
> You cretinous, senile old fart!
> Thanks to you, we're to be thrown to
> the Turks!

A shell explodes nearby and SALT, SALLY the BARON and
the others duck back into the comparative shelter of
the foyer of the theater.

                      SALLY
                    (excited)
He really is Baron Munchausen! ...
The real one!

                      SALT
                    (distraught)
Oh, shut up!

                      SALLY
But he is! And he can save us! ...
                    (to the BARON)
Can't you?

                      BARON
                    (looking
                    clapped-out)
Er ...

                      SALLY
                    (enthusiastically)
I know! You could escape — find your
funny servants and bring them back to
rescue us.
                    (excited)
He jumped onto a cannonball ... he
really did ... and flew away miles
into the sky ... up above the
elephants and soldiers ... and ...

                      SALT
Oh God! Stop lying!

                      SALLY
I'm not lying!
                    (triumphant, to the
                    BARON)
Am I?!

                      BARON
As a matter of fact, you are.

                      SALLY
                    (stunned by this
                    "betrayal")
But you did! ... And those soldiers
saw it too!
                    (MORE)

                                 (CONTINUED)

>               SALLY (CONT.)
>                 (to SALT)
>         They'll tell you! ...
>                 (recalling the
>                 scene)
>         Oh ... they're dead.

>                 SALT
>                 (groans)

>                 SALLY
>         But he did.

>                 BARON
>         No, I didn't!

>                 SALLY
>                 (furious)
>         Now *you're* lying!

>                 BARON
>                 (starchily)
>         I never lie.

SALLY, seething with rage, kicks the BARON and runs off into the theater to hide her tears. BILL, JEREMY, RUPERT and DESMOND look accusingly at the BARON.

>                 BARON
>                 (exhausted but
>                 pedantic to the end)
>         I didn't "*fly miles*." It was more
>         like a mile and a half. And I didn't
>         precisely "fly," I merely held onto a
>         mortar shell in the first instance
>         and *then* a cannonball on the way
>         back.

>                 SALT
>         You maniac! You've done for us!

The DOG growls at SALT

>                 BARON
>         Actually, it doesn't matter whether
>         you're thrown out or stay here. The
>         Turks are about to take the town.

EVERYBODY looks in horror at the BARON. They don't quite know whether to believe him.

(CONTINUED)

                              SALT
                        (breaking down)
                And I'm just coming into my prime.
                Just on the cusp between Romeo and
                King Lear! ... My public will kill me
                for dying at a time like this.

At this point, we hear the desperate shouting and the
noise of soldiers moving cannon on gun-carriages. SALT
& CO. look out through the hole in the theater wall.

                                                    CUT TO:

SALT AND CO.'s P.O.V. where we see the desperate
activity of SOLDIERS trundling cannons past the
theater towards a breech somewhere in the defenses.
Trumpets are sounding the call to arms.

ANGLE ON SALT & CO. as VIOLET, ROSE and DAISY throw
themselves at the BARON.

                              DAISY
                        (clutching the BARON
                        and baby)
                Save us! Save us!

                              ROSE
                Please, Baron!

                              VIOLET
                        (pleading)
                Baron, you are a Baron, aren't you?

                              DAISY
                You're our only hope!

                              VIOLET
                You're *my* only hope!

                              BARON
                Ladies, ladies ... please ... please.

The BARON, suddenly surrounded at close proximity by
distraught women, is overcome by something which
sublimates itself in chivalry.

                              BARON
                ...  I swear that as long as I,
                Hieronymous Karl Friedrich, Baron von
                        (MORE)

                                            (CONTINUED)

                         BARON (CONT.)
          Munchausen ... live and breathe, you
          shall come to no harm.

                         VIOLET
          Oh yes ... Oh yes ... Say it again.

                         SALT
                    (contemptuously)
          Ha!

The BARON produces red paper roses from inside his
jacket and presents one each to VIOLET, ROSE and
DAISY.

                         BARON
                    (presenting roses)
          You so remind me of Catherine the
          Great, the Empress of all the
          Russias, whose hand in marriage I
          once had the honor to decline.

                         DESMOND
          They all remind you?

                         BARON
          Yes. Why not? Some bits here, some
          bits there.
                    (grandly)
          I have a plan ... I will set forth
          immediately ...

The BARON pulls his saber from its scabbard and tries
to flourish it, but in so doing, falls over from
weakness and exhaustion.

                         BARON
                    (from the floor)
          ... find my extraordinary servants,
          and with their help, raise the siege
          and save the town.

                         SALT
                    (sarcastically)
          Oh, brilliant, very good, bravo.

                         DAISY
          How?

(CONTINUED)

                    BARON
          Ladies, I shall require your
          assistance.

                    VIOLET
          Of course.

                    DAISY
          Anything.

                    ROSE
          Just tell us what to do.

                    BARON
          Kindly be so good as to remove your
          knickers.


34 EXT.        **ON FORESTAGE IN THEATER**        **DAWN**

We are looking at a pile of material which is moving
and writhing around in an odd sort of way.

The CAMERA PULLS BACK to reveal that we on the
forestage of the theater, and that the material is
hundreds of pieces of silk underwear which have been
sewn together to make a balloon. The balloon is
attached by ropes to the miniature galleon which
becomes a gondola.

There is a small brazier in the crow's nest of the
galleon from where the BARON is working bellows which
are blowing hot air into the balloon. The BARON is
very lively and seems much rejuvenated by this
undertaking. The DOG is leaping excitedly about the
galleon. The theater COMPANY are holding the guide
ropes of the balloon, keeping it clear of
entanglement, and waiting for it to rise. The
auditorium is full of TOWNSPEOPLE watching the
proceedings. Outside, at the walls and gates of the
town, the Turkish attack continues.

                    DESMOND
               (ecstatic, looking
                up at the balloon)
          Look at all that underwear. Isn't it
          beautiful? It's like a dream come
          true. It's the dawning of the age of
          ... lovely, intimate things.

                                        (CONTINUED)

> BILL
> But it's madness. He'll kill himself.

The BARON continues to fill the balloon with hot air.

> DESMOND
> Yes, but well worth it, eh?

JEREMY and RUPERT are holding onto ropes from the balloon.

> JEREMY
> How do we know he isn't just saving his own skin, eh?

> RUPERT
> Oh, shut up!

> JEREMY
> It's only because he's tall, isn't it? I mean, let's face it — if he was a foot shorter this wouldn't be happening.

> RUPERT
> Be quiet!

> JEREMY
> (getting angry)
> And if he was *two* feet shorter his tales would be all about how he spent his life in fairy-land, with other little people, down some whimsical chocolate mine!

ANGLE ON ROSE and DAISY.

> DAISY
> (wistfully looking
> up towards the
> BARON)
> Can you trust a man who makes balloons out of underwear?

> BARON
> Trust me, madam. Your underwear is in good hands.

ANGLE ON VIOLET.

(CONTINUED)

                              VIOLET
                        (shouting at the
                          BARON)
                   I'll wait for you!


35  EXT.      **HOLE IN AUDITORIUM WALL**      **DAWN**

    Two SOLDIERS are watching the activity on stage with
    suspicion. They exchange looks.


36  EXT.      **SQUARE**      **DAWN**

    The two SOLDIERS hurry away across the square.


37  INT.      **THE COUNCIL CHAMBER**      **TOWN HALL**      **DAWN**

    In the council chamber, HORATIO JACKSON and his
    FUNCTIONARIES continue to conduct the war. They have
    been up all night, and are exhausted.

                          JACKSON
                      (discarding plans)
                   No, no, no ... We need a very simple
                   plan. These are far too complicated.
                   Simplicity is of the essence.

    FUNCTIONARIES look puzzled.

    A COLONEL enters. The two SOLDIERS we saw in the
    square wait outside the door.

                          COLONEL
                   Sir ... Sir, those actors have made
                   an air balloon. They're trying to
                   escape.

                          JACKSON
                   Arrest them at once. Throw them out
                   of the town.

                          COLONEL
                   We can't open the gates, sir.

                          JACKSON
                   Well, throw them over the walls then.


                                              (CONTINUED)

                              COLONEL
            Yes, sir.

The COLONEL exits.

                              JACKSON
            We can't start escaping at a time
            like this ... What would future
            generations think of us.

38  INT.      THEATER AUDITORIUM      DAWN

The BARON gives the balloon a final couple of blasts
from the bellows, providing it with sufficient air to
lift it off the stage. The balloon then lifts gently
into position above the galleon which is still
stationary. Everybody is very excited, and the
AUDIENCE cheers as the balloon begins to float. The
galleon swings into position, knocking a couple of
already-wounded members of the audience over.

39  EXT.      TOWN SQUARE        DAWN

The COLONEL and a group of GUARDS are racing across
the square towards the theater.

40  INT.      IN FRONT OF THE THEATER      DAWN

The BARON gives the balloon another couple of blasts
of hot air, causing it to lift the galleon just clear
of the fore-stage. The balloon with its gondola is now
straining at the ropes, and the ACTORS are having
difficulty hanging onto it. ROSE climbs a ladder
leaning against the galleon. SALT rushes on from
backstage.

                              SALT
                          (fraught)
            Oy! Have you seen Sally?

                              BARON
                       (operating bellows)
            No!

At this point the COLONEL and his GUARDS run into the
auditorium.

(CONTINUED)

>               COLONEL
>     Stop! ... You're under arrest!

The COLONEL and GUARDS begin pushing their way through
the AUDIENCE towards the balloon. The BARON sees them
coming.

>               BARON
>            (heaving out
>            ballast)
>     Let her go! ... Let her go! ...
>            (he doffs his hat to
>            ROSE)

The ACTORS let go of the ropes, and the balloon slowly
begins to rise, taking the galleon with it.

>               COLONEL
>            (to GUARDS)
>     Shoot it down!
>            (raising his saber)
>     Take aim!

The GUARDS raise their muskets and take aim at the
balloon whereupon ARGUS jumps from the gondola, runs
to the COLONEL and leaps at him. The COLONEL falls
back, knocking over the GUARDS domino fashion. Their
muskets go off harmlessly into the air.

>               BARON
>            (shouting down to
>            the AUDIENCE)
>     Ladies and gentlemen, I will return
>     shortly with re-inforcements. Don't
>     lose heart. And for all those ladies
>     to whom I am indebted, for half a ton
>     of frilly silk and lacy linen — don't
>     catch cold. Au revoir.

The balloon begins to gain height. ARGUS barks up at
his master.

>               BARON
>     Stay, Argus. Stay! I'll soon be back.


41  INT.        THE COUNCIL CHAMBER - TOWN HALL     DAWN

ANGLE ON a furious JACKSON and his FUNCTIONARIES as
they watch the balloon and galleon rise out of the

(CONTINUED)

hole in the theater roof. It floats across the square
with its ruined church.

>                    JACKSON
>           He won't get far on hot air and
>           fantasy.

**42 EXT.   WITH THE BARON IN THE GALLEON     EARLY MORNING**

The BARON raises his hat in a florid and gracious
salute to JACKSON and begins to jettison another sack
of ballast. Suddenly, out of the sack topples SALLY.
He grabs for her but it is too late. She falls away
from him to her certain death.

The BARON looks down, horrified, only to discover that
she has snagged onto the anchor which is suspended
below the galleon on a length of rope.

The BARON hauls her back up into the galleon.

>                    SALLY
>               (scared but trying
>               not to show it)
>           Thanks.

>                    BARON
>               (picking up a
>               container of water)
>           You've ruined everything! ... I'll
>           have to douse the fire to put you
>           down! ... I'll never get off again!
>           ...

>                    SALLY
>               (stepping between
>               the BARON and the
>               brazier)
>           I'm going with you!

>                    BARON
>           No you're not!

>                    SALLY
>           I am!

>                    BARON
>           I absolutely and utterly refuse!

(CONTINUED)

> SALLY
> (pointing down,
> triumphant)
> If we go down now, we'll land on the
> Turks.

CUT TO:

THE BARON'S P.O.V. as he looks over the side of the
galleon just in time to see them pass over the
battlements and drift out over the Turkish camp. A
fierce battle is taking place all along the walls as
the TURKS storm the town.

> SALLY
> (looking at the
> fighting)
> We've got to find your servants and
> get back here quickly!

ANGLE ON the BARON peering through a telescope at a
pale crescent moon (normal size), above them.

> BARON
> (irritated)
> That *is* what I had in mind.

> SALLY
> Where are we going?

> BARON
> To the moon.

> SALLY
> What? . . . That'll take ages!

> BARON
> No it won't.

> SALLY
> Of course it will!

The BARON gives SALLY an exasperated look.

> SALLY
> Why are we going there?

> BARON
> That's where I last saw Berthold.
> Have you ever been to the moon?

(CONTINUED)

56

                          SALLY

       No.


                          BARON

       Ah! Interesting place. The King and
       Queen are charming. You know about
       their detachable heads don't you?

                          SALLY

       No.


                          BARON

       Ah. Yes. Moonlings can send their
       heads off separately for intellectual
       pursuits, while their bodies engage in
       more ... bodily activities. Trouble
       is, their heads and bodies don't
       always see eye to eye.

SALLY looks skeptical.

                          BARON
                     (mischievously)
       You do believe me, don't you?

                          SALLY
                       (wary)
       I'm doing my best.

The BARON smiles.


43  **EXT.**      **IN THE GALLEON**     **NIGHT**

The balloon is in the middle of a raging storm. Rain
is pouring down, threatening to put out the fire in
the brazier. Thunder and lightning are rolling and
flashing all around. The galleon is really being
thrown about. SALLY and the BARON are clinging to the
rigging. In front of them is the crescent moon. It
seems unnaturally large.

                          SALLY
                   (above the noise of
                    the wind)
       Are you scared?

                          BARON
                    (terrified)
       Certainly not! Are you?


                            57

                         SALLY
                      (terrified)
              Certainly not!

Suddenly a bolt of lightning blasts through the
rigging, severing the ropes connecting the galleon to
the balloon. The balloon in immediately blown off into
space, leaving the galleon spinning and lurching on
into the storm. The rain has now begun to behave like
the sea, splashing up over the prow of the galleon
which in turn has begun to move up and down as if on
waves. The OLD SOLDIER and the LITTLE GIRL struggle
together to gain control of their tiny craft as the
monstrous storm hurls them onward. The crescent moon,
in front of them, is now gigantic, filling nearly all
of the sky and getting bigger. The storm begins to
subside. Soon the galleon is sailing through a calm
sea. This sea seems to drain away — sink into sand —
until all the water has vanished and the boat is
plying its way across what appears to be a desert ...
the sand behaving like water.


**44  EXT.    SEA OF TRANQUILITY**

In the little galleon the BARON lies exhausted,
asleep. The BARON's arm hangs over the side — his
fingers dragging in what now is definitely sand. He
wakes, to find SALLY alert and ready to go.

                         SALLY
                      (enthusiastic)
              We're here! You look different ...
              younger.

                         BARON
              I always feel rejuvenated by a touch
              of adventure. For heaven's sake, don't
              *you* get any younger ... or I'll have
              to find a wet nurse.


**45  APPROACHING STRUCTURE ON MOON    DAY**

The BARON and SALLY sail, in the galleon, across the
sea of sand, towards a gigantic, open, metal,
spherical structure (similar to an orrery) which lies
imbedded in the ground. Through the great metal bands
that compose this construction we can see the horizon
... except for one particular section that seems to

(CONTINUED)

have part of a building inside. The BARON and SALLY
sail directly towards this.

> BARON
> You'll find that I'm one of the King's
> special favorites. We'll receive a
> right royal welcome.

The moment that the BARON and SALLY sail into the
interior of the gigantic sphere, the small building
towards which they were heading is revealed to part of
a huge impressive city. To make matters stranger, the
buildings disassemble as they glide through them.
Parts that appear to be distant prove to be in the
foreground. Walls that seem to be at right angles to
them are revealed to be at 45 degrees. Gigantic stone
bases are in fact tiny pebbles directly in front of
SALLY's nose. As they enter the city they hear the
sound of welcoming brass bands and cheering crowds.
SALLY looks around for the source of this noise but
can't see any sign of life. She appeals to the BARON
who smiles, shrugs, and begins to wave to the
invisible crowd. SALLY obviously thinks that this is
quite daft. They sail through this insubstantial city
until they approach what seems to be the palace. A
magnificent building rising at the end of a long
avenue of equally impressive buildings. The music and
cheering reach a crescendo as they suddenly, to their
surprise, bump into the palace, which in fact, is just
a painted cutout slightly taller than their boat. The
buildings on either side of them are equally false,
flat and pressing right up against the sides of the
boat. A noise behind them spins them around and they
see a fourth wall of buildings closing behind them.
SALLY looks around in alarm and then in fear as she
sees a gigantic floating head loom up over the wall.
It belongs to the KING OF THE MOON.

> KING'S HEAD
> (his face straining
> and contorting)
> I've got you at last. Bienvenu alla
> luna, Baron.

> BARON
> Your Majesty. What a great pleasure it
> is to see you again. May I introduce
> my friend, Sally. Sally, the King of
> the Moon. Well, his head at any rate.

(CONTINUED)

>                    KING'S HEAD
> I'm sorry, but I must insist on the
> correct title. King of *Everything*. Ray
> Di Tutto, but you can call me Ray. You
> know, the moon is a very insignificant
> part of my domain now. There is so
> much much much much much much more.

The KING'S FACE goes into a spasm of straining and
contorting.

>                    BARON
> My old friend, you seem to be in some
> discomfort. What ails you?

>                    KING'S HEAD
>                   (irritated)
> Nothing ails me! Can you not see that
> I am one with the cosmos?

>                    BARON
> Ah.

>                    KING'S HEAD
> Ah? I tell you that and all you can
> say is "Ah"? What, are you blind?
> Baron, let me explain to you.
>                   (straining)
> Since you were last here, I, that is,
> my head, that which is left of me,
> where the brilliant and important
> parts are located, is now ruling and
> governing the known universe. And that
> which I don't know, I create.
>                   (he whistles)
> I just created spring. Without me,
> there would be nothing, not even you
> ... "Cogito ergo es": I think,
> therefore you is.

The BARON and SALLY exchange looks.

>                    SALLY
> Your old friend's a lunatic.

>                    BARON
>                   (annoyed)
> Without my *adventures* you wouldn't be
> here.

(CONTINUED)

>                    KING'S HEAD
>                    (triumphant)
>           So, I'm now part of your "adventures"
>           am I? Well, we shall see about that,
>           huh.

The KING'S HEAD thinks hard.

.

CUT TO:

THE BARON AND SALLY. Their surroundings have suddenly
changed. The galleon and the walls of the city have
disappeared, and they now find themselves, surrounded
with splendid drawing-room furniture and fittings,
stuck on top of a tall plinth. In effect, in a
comfortable prison.

ANGLE ON the KING'S HEAD which is hovering in space
beside the plinth.

>                    KING'S HEAD
>           Who created who? I hope you'll be very
>           comfortable. Ciao!

In the background, middle distance, we see the QUEEN
and the KING'S BODY pass across the landscape. They
are making rude noises and the KING'S BODY is
clutching the QUEEN. The QUEEN is carrying a butterfly
net.

>                    KING'S HEAD
>           There goes my revolting body with the
>           Queen. It's so embarrassing. Please
>           don't look! Maybe he will go away.
>           It's hard to believe my body and I
>           were ever attached, we are so
>           incompatible. I mean, he is still
>           dangling from the food chain and I am
>           in the stars ... oh, it is so
>           unmetaphysical!

As the KING'S HEAD speaks a HAND reaches up from
below, grabs the head and pulls it down.

>                    KING'S HEAD
>           No, no, go away! I despise you, let me
>           go! No, no, no!

ANGLE ON the KING and QUEEN standing beside the
plinth. The KING'S BODY is still clutching at the

(CONTINUED)

QUEEN with one hand while forcing his head back onto his
body with his other hand. Attached to his belt is a sack
of food. At the moment when the KING'S HEAD and BODY are
reunited the KING seems to undergo a change of
personality.

>                    KING (reunited)
>                    (belches)
>          I'm back! I've got my lips again
>                    (to QUEEN)
>          and I'm going to use them, baby. It's
>          me — I'm your elephant of joy. Let me
>          bite you, baby.
>                    (laughs)

>                    QUEEN
>          Eat first, darling.

>                    KING
>          That's right, you got to "muncha
>          before you bitecha"!

CLOSE ON the KING holding his head onto his body and
stuffing food into his mouth.

>                    KING
>                    (eating)
>          Mmm! Better! Better!
>                    (hitting his head)
>          Pretentious, namby pamby head!

ANGLE ON the BARON, who has caught the QUEEN's eye.

>                    BARON
>                    (doffing hat to
>                    QUEEN)
>          Your most wondrous Majesty ...

>                    KING
>                    (interrupting)
>          I know you! You're the little guy who
>          tried to take off with my queen last
>          time you were here. We have no more of
>          that — piccolo casanova!

>                                        CUT TO:

THE BARON and SALLY who are now not in the
"comfortable" prison, but in a rough straw-filled
cage, suspended in space.

>                                   (CONTINUED)

45 CONTINUED:

ANGLE ON KING and QUEEN.

                    KING
               (holding head on)
          There you go, love birds. I'm sure
          you'll be very uncomfortable.

At this point, after a brief struggle, the KING's HEAD
escapes from his body.

                 KING'S HEAD
              (spitting out food)
          I am free again. Free to concentrate
          on higher things!

The KING'S BODY jumps up and down with rage. It throws
food, blindly, in the direction of the KING'S HEAD
which is once more straining to exercise its will
power, while sticking out its tongue at its enraged
body.

                 KING'S HEAD
               (dodging food
                missiles)
          Troglodyte! I'm trying to concentrate
          on higher things! Go and amuse
          yourself in the slime!

A butterfly net comes up from below and captures the
HEAD which it drags down out of shot.

                 KING'S HEAD
          No! No! Let me go! I've got things to
          do! Tides to regulate! Comets to
          direct! I haven't got time for bodily
          functions or black leather posing
          briefs.


46  INT.   CAGE ON MOON

ANGLE ON the cage suspended from below (world upside
down) in a space which may or may not be recognizable
as a cell, depending upon construction material
already available. The cage contains the BARON and
SALLY and a large pile of straw in the middle.

                    SALLY
                 (furious)
          "One of the King's favorites?"


                      63

                              BARON
             I can't understand it.

                              SALLY
             He said the last time you were here
             you tried to make off with his Queen.
             Doesn't that ring a bell?

                              BARON
             It's quite untrue. I er ... I was
             merely polite to her.

SALLY looks at the BARON with disgust.

                              BARON
             I'm afraid the "King of Everything"
             has little regard for facts. Let this
             be a warning to you.

                              SALLY
                          (surly)
             What do you mean?

                              BARON
             This is the fate of those who ignore
             the truth.

                              SALLY
             What is?

                              BARON
             To end up ...

                              SALLY
                          (accusingly)
             ... In a cage on the moon?

                              BARON
             This cage isn't real. It's just part
             of the King's lunacy.

                              SALLY
                          (kicking bar)
             Seems strong enough to me.

                              BARON
                          (put out)
             I see we're in a not very helpful
             frame of mind.

                                              (CONTINUED)

> SALLY
> How are we supposed to save the town
> from here?

> BARON
> (embarrassed)
> The town's perfectly all right. The
> present assault is over. Everyone
> there is quite safe.

> SALLY
> How do you know?

> BARON
> I just know.

**47 EXT.      THE CITY      DAY**

A very quick scene of ferocious hand-to-hand fighting
along the city walls as waves of TURKS swarm up
ladders and over the battlements and attack the
DEFENDERS.

**48 BACK IN THE CAGE ON THE MOON**

SALLY is looking at the BARON skeptically. She kicks
at the pile of straw lying on the floor of the cage.

> VOICE
> (from under straw)
> Ow!

The BARON draws his saber.

> BARON
> Come out! ... Come out of there!

The BARON prods the straw with his saber.

> VOICE
> Ow! Stop that!

An OLD MAN with white hair and funny teeth emerges
from under the straw.

> OLD MAN
> (indignant)
> What'd you do that for?!!!

(CONTINUED)

> BARON
>
> I beg your pardon, I thought you might
> be unfriendly.

> OLD MAN
>
> Of course I'm unfriendly! You'd be
> unfriendly if I prodded you!

> SALLY
>
> Who are you?

> OLD MAN
> (thinks)
> I can't remember. I've been here so
> long.

> SALLY
>
> We'll be like that if we don't escape.

> BARON
>
> Why are you here?

> OLD MAN
>
> Oh, I'm a very wicked criminal.

> SALLY
>
> What have you done?

> OLD MAN
>
> I can't remember

> SALLY
>
> Then how do you know you're very
> wicked?

> OLD MAN
>
> Well, for one thing ... I'm in here.
> And for another ... I've got these
> shackles on.

The OLD MAN steps out of the straw dragging shackles
with him. These are in fact BERTHOLD's weights.

> BARON
> (excited)
> Berthold!!!

> BERTHOLD
> (to SALLY)
> Eh?

(CONTINUED)

                        BARON
                      (to SALLY)
                  It's Berthold!!!

The BARON leaps forward and embraces BERTHOLD.
(BERTHOLD is played, once again, by DESMOND from
Salt's theater company, but this time not in heavy
theatrical make-up. In other words he is more "real"
as BERTHOLD than he was in the Sultan's Tale. He is
also much older.)

                        BARON
                  Berthold! It's me! ... The Baron! I
                  knew I'd find you on the moon! We're
                  going to take you back to earth, to
                  help us fight the Sultan.

BERTHOLD tries to fight off the BARON's embraces.

                        BERTHOLD
                  Get off! ... Get off me! ...

                        BARON
                  You're Berthold, Berthold my old
                  servant. Those leg irons are to slow
                  you down ... Stop you tearing off all
                  over the place ...

                        BERTHOLD
                  You must be joking.

                        BARON
                  You always wore them ... Remember?

                        BERTHOLD
                  You're crackers.

                        BARON
                  I'm Baron Munchausen.

                        BERTHOLD
                  That sounds nasty. Is it contagious?

                        SALLY
                  We're wasting time!

                        ARIADNE (V.O.)
                      (sexily)
                  Baron.

(CONTINUED)

The BARON, SALLY, and BERTHOLD look towards the direction of the voice.

ANOTHER ANGLE ON the cage as ARIADNE's HEAD hovers into view.

> BARON
> (delighted)
> Ariadne?

> ARIADNE
> (key to cage in her
> mouth)
> Darling Baron. I'm sorry I couldn't
> speak to you before but Roger's so
> difficult.

ARIADNE unlocks the door of the cage by inserting the key into the lock with her teeth and rotating her head 360 degrees.

> ARIADNE
> (opening the cage
> door still with
> teeth)
> You're much too handsome to languish
> in a cage.

> BARON
> (forced casual)
> Where exactly is Roger?

> ARIADNE
> He's in bed with my body.
> (orgasmic)
> Oooooh ... Stop it! ... But if he
> discovers that my head's with you ...
> Ahhh ... Quickly, climb into my hair!
> Ooooaaahh! Oooooaaaeee!

ARIADNE positions her head against the open door of the cage.

> SALLY
> (aside to BARON)
> Why is she making those funny noises?

(CONTINUED)

> BARON
> (embarrassed)
> Her body's with the King and ... he's
> tickling her feet.
> (turning quickly to
> Berthold)
> Berthold!

The BARON drags BERTHOLD out of the pile of giant
straw.

> BARON
>
> Come on!

> BERTHOLD
> (struggling)
> Let go of me! ...

> BARON
> You're coming with us.

> BERTHOLD
>
> No chance!

> BARON
>
> Why not?

> BERTHOLD
> (thinks)
> Can't remember.

> BARON
> You're not frightened, are you?

> BERTHOLD
>
> That's it!

> BARON
> (to SALLY)
> Help me.

The BARON and SALLY bundle the struggling BERTHOLD out
of the cage and onto ARIADNE's head where they cling
to her hair and crown.

ARIADNE'S HEAD with the BARON and CO. on board then
zooms out of shot.

**EXT.**        **MOONSCAPE**        **DAY**

A moonscape full of abandoned, half-finished buildings
and structures. The QUEEN'S HEAD zooms across it,
carrying the BARON, SALLY, and BERTHOLD.

>                    ARIADNE
>     Oh oh oh oh aaaah. Ooooooh!

                                              CUT TO:

THE BARON, SALLY AND BERTHOLD as they climb down from
ARIADNE'S HEAD.

>                    ARIADNE
>     Ah, ah, ah, aaaaaah! Oh, Baron, I must
>     get back to Roger before he notices
>     I'm headless.

>                    BARON
>     I quite understand.

>                    ARIADNE
>                 (suddenly
>                 passionate)
>     Darling ... take me with you!

>                    BARON
>                 (taken aback)
>     My dear ... Back to earth?

>                    ARIADNE
>     Yes.

>                    BARON
>     Er ... Without your body?

>                    ARIADNE
>                 (hurt)
>     I thought you loved me for myself?

>                    BARON
>     Oh, I did, I mean I do, of course I
>     do. It's just that ...

>                    SALLY
>                 (sick of this)
>     We've got to go!

                                          (CONTINUED)

                    ARIADNE
          No, you're right, it's impossible ...
          it was just a mad thought ... Here ...
          take a lock of my hair.

The BARON takes out his saber and cuts a six-foot lock
of ARIADNE's hair which he ties around his neck like a
long scarf.

                    BERTHOLD
          Just a lock, cocky! Not the whole
          carpet!

                    BARON
          I shall treasure it, always.

                    ARIADNE
          Ooooooooooooh ... ! Aaaaaaaaaaaah ... !
          The King's ... Haaaaaaaaaaaaaaaaa ... !
          I must go back. OOOOOOOOOOOH ... ! Au
          revoir dear Baron ... AAAAAAAAAAAH ...!
          OO, OO, OO, OO, AAH! Good luck!
          AAAAAAAAAAH!

The BARON plucks a red paper rose from inside his
jacket and puts it between ARIADNE's teeth.

ARIADNE'S HEAD zooms out of shot.

REVERSE ANGLE ON ARIADNE'S HEAD as it shoots away from
the BARON, SALLY and BERTHOLD.

                    ARIADNE
          I'm coming Roger, I'm coming.
          OOOOOOOOAAAAAAAAOOOOOOO ... !

50  INT.    KING'S BEDROOM    DAY

The KING is tickling the QUEEN's feet. The QUEEN's
body is moving under the bedclothes.

                    KING
          Ticky, ticky, ticky, ticky,  ... etc.

The KING crawls under the bedclothes at the bottom end
of the bed and begins to move up towards where the
QUEEN's head should be. KING is holding his head on.

(CONTINUED)

>                   KING
>             (under bedclothes)
>     Ticky, ticky, ticky, ticky ...

The KING suddenly stops and sticks his head out of the
side of the covers.

>                   KING
>     What's up with you today? Not a peep,
>     not a murmur! You're about as
>     responsive as a dead haddock! Don't
>     tell me you've got another headache!
>     Eh? ... There's nothing wrong with my
>     tickling, girl, I can tell you that!
>     I'm as good as ever! Better! I'm
>     tickling now, longer, stronger, more
>     effectively than I ever was! Practice
>     makes perfect ... Give us a kiss.

The KING continues under the covers until he reaches
the QUEEN's headless neck.

>                   KING
>     Good god, where's your head?!
>             (he rummages in the
>             bedclothes)
>     You can't have a headache without a
>     head.
>             (sudden realization)
>     It's with the Baron, isn't it?! I'll
>     kill him! I'll tear him to shreds!

The KING snatches the arm of an eighteenth century
record/disc/cylinder music box which instantly
silences the moon muzak which has been playing until
this moment.

>                   KING
>     Fetch me my radish club and celery
>     sword! ... Rats, they're out of
>     season! OK, OK, bring the asparagus
>     spear! The deadliest vegetable in my
>     arsenal! I'll teach the bounder!
>             (pause)
>     Fine, fine, I'll get it myself! Who am
>     I kidding! Not only are there no
>     servants here, but they're all totally
>     incompetent! SILVER! SILVER! TIME FOR
>     DINNER!

                                    (CONTINUED)

At this point, Terry Gilliam does his vocal impression of giant griffin and a GIANT, TALONED GRIFFIN foot smashes through the door, window or wall (depending upon what's available from what has already been built).

                    KING
        Mind the paintwork! You clumsy brute!


**51  EXT.      MOONSCAPE      DAY**

THE BARON AND CO. struggle across the moon, away from the palace, past the abandoned, half-finished buildings and structures. We hear the blast of a distant hunting horn. The BARON and CO. look back towards the directions of the palace.

                                        CUT TO:

THE BARON AND CO.'S P.O.V. where we see, hovering over the palace, a mounted THREE-HEADED GRIFFIN.

                                        CUT TO:

A CLOSEUP of the GRIFFIN which we discover is being ridden by the KING, armed with a mushroom shield and asparagus spear.

                    KING
                (steadying the
                griffin)
        Hungry are we, Silver? Well, down
        there are three tasty wee snacks. Go
        get 'em!

The KING spurs the GRIFFIN, which roars, rears back and then zooms away with much snarling of flared nostrils and beating of wings.

                                        CUT TO:

THE BARON AND CO. as they try to run faster.

                    BARON
        Faster!

                    SALLY
                (frantic)
        We can't! Berthold can hardly move!

                                        (CONTINUED)

> BARON
> Take his weights off!

> SALLY
> I have!

> BARON
> (puzzled)
> What?

The BARON looks at BERTHOLD who is indeed without his weights.

> SALLY
> He's old! He can't run any more!

> BARON
> Nonsense! He's just out of practice!
> Come on, Berthold!

SALLY glances back towards the fast gaining GRIFFIN.

> SALLY
> (scared)
> It's going to catch us!

ANGLE ON the KING as he spurs on the GRIFFIN and raises and throws his asparagus spear.

ANGLE ON the BARON and CO., who are now moving a tiny bit faster, as the asparagus spear shoots overhead and thumps into the ground just in front of BERTHOLD. BERTHOLD, glancing fearfully back at the approaching GRIFFIN, runs smack into the quivering asparagus spear and knocks himself out. The BARON and SALLY stop running and return the few steps to try and help BERTHOLD. At this point they fall into the shadow of the noisy GRIFFIN.

ANGLE ON the KING as the maddened, starving GRIFFIN goes into a dive.

ANGLE ON the BARON and CO. as the BARON signals to SALLY that he wants her to run in one direction while he intends to run in the other.

CUT TO:

A WIDE SHOT of the scene in which the BARON and SALLY run in opposite directions leaving the unconscious

(CONTINUED)

BERTHOLD in the middle. The GRIFFIN's heads fan out,
each one following a different potential meal. The
KING tries desperately to control them.

> KING
> Whoa! Together! Together! Teamwork!
> Teamwork!

The out-of-control GRIFFIN is stretching, straining,
shuddering until its body can no longer hold itself
together. RIP! SPRONG! ZIP! POP! BOING! The GRIFFIN
comes apart! Springs, gears, all sorts of clockwork
mechanism fly out. One head and wing spiral up and
away. Feathers fill the air. What remains of the body
— with the KING frantically trying to rein it in —
hurtles to the ground. On impact the KING'S head
bounces and shoots off into space.

> KING'S HEAD
> (receding fast)
> Free! Free! At last! The body's dead!
> Finished! I can concentrate on my
> great task! Pure thought! A head can
> live without a body, can't it? I shall
> prove it! I shall definitely prove it.
> One doesn't have to *have* to wash one's
> hair!

The KING'S HEAD disappears. As the feathers and dust
clear, SALLY and the BARON make their way back to
BERTHOLD as he regains consciousness.

> BERTHOLD
> (recovering)
> Baron! Baron Munchausen!

BERTHOLD embraces the BARON, who has to fight him off.

> BERTHOLD
> It's great to see you! What are you
> doing here?

> BARON
> (pushing him away)
> Let go of me.

> BERTHOLD
> It's Berthold — Berthold. Your old
> servant. Remember?

(CONTINUED)

> BARON
> (tetchily)
> Yes, yes. We've been through all that.

> BERTHOLD
> Oh! Where are we?

> SALLY
> On the moon.

> BERTHOLD
> Oh yeah? Same old Baron, eh?

> SALLY
> Can we go now?

> BARON
> (giving some of
> Ariadne's hair to
> Sally)
> Get weaving.

> BERTHOLD
> Hang on, hang on, it's all coming
> back. I've been stuck here for over
> twenty years ... since the last time
> you were on the moon! You abandoned me
> here! You swine! You toddled off with
> the Queen of tarts and left me to rot
> in that parrot cage, didn't you?! And
> now you come back when it suits you,
> having wasted half my life, and expect
> me to follow you to the ends of the
> earth.

> BARON
> Yes.

> BERTHOLD
> Oh, all right.

They move off. BERTHOLD with difficulty.


52 **EXT.**    **CRESCENT MOON**

The BARON and CO. move across the moonscape towards
what has now become the horn of a crescent moon,
weaving Ariadne's hair as they go.

**53 EXT.    TIP OF CRESCENT MOON**

The BARON and CO. reach the point of the crescent.
They have to balance carefully to avoid falling off.
By now, Ariadne's hair has become a recognizable rope.

The BARON attaches one end of the rope to the horn,
and drops the rest of it into the abyss.

> BARON
> Berthold, you go first. Then you,
> Sally.

BERTHOLD and SALLY, followed by the BARON, slip off
the edge of the crescent moon and climb down the hair
rope into space.

> BARON
> Berthold? Do you know where the rest
> of the gang are?

> BERTHOLD
> Not a clue.

**54 EXT.    ROPE IN SPACE**

ANGLE ON the bottom end of the hair rope as it dangles
in space. After a moment BERTHOLD climbs down to it.

> BERTHOLD
> (shouting up
> hysterically)
> That's it! Finito! There's no more
> rope! Mind out! I'm coming back up!

> BARON (V.O.)
> (from above)
> Wait a moment!
> (pause)
> Here! Tie this to it!

Another end of rope is passed down to BERTHOLD.

> BERTHOLD
> (puzzled, examining
> the rope)
> Where'd you get this from?

(CONTINUED)

>                         BARON (V.O.)
>             I untied it from the top.

>                         BERTHOLD
>                     (confused)
>             From the top?

>                         BARON (V.O.)
>             Naturally ... Where else do you think
>             I'd get it from?

>                         BERTHOLD
>             But ...

>                         BARON (V.O.)
>                     (exasperated)
>             Yes yes yes ... Hurry up and splice it
>             to the bottom, so that we may continue
>             our descent!

>                         BERTHOLD
>             Oh, very clever. Great. Why didn't I
>             think of that!
>                     (to SALLY)
>             That's why he's a Baron and I'm a
>             prole.

                                                    CUT TO:

A WIDE SHOT of the BARON and CO. climbing down the
rope. Far below them, in the blackness of space, is
the earth's sphere.

ANGLE ON SALLY as she slides down the fraying hair
rope.

>                         SALLY
>             The rope's fraying!

ANGLE ON BERTHOLD as the rope comes apart in his
hands.

>                         BERTHOLD
>             I'll say! Ahhhhhhh!

BERTHOLD falls out of frame, followed by SALLY and the
BARON.

55  EXT.      BARON AND CO. FALL THROUGH SPACE

The BARON and CO. fall through space towards the
planet Earth which appears to be increasing in size
beneath them.

                    SALLY
                  (terrified)
        We'll never rescue them now, will we?!

They continue towards the Earth on which we see a
volcano from where smoke is pouring.

56  INT. VULCAN'S WORKSHOP INSIDE THE VOLCANO

A vast cavernous rock chamber inside the volcano at
one end of which is a large open blacksmith's furnace.
There is no blazing fire in the furnace and all the
machinery is still. Surrounding the furnace are anvils
and workbenches with racks of hammers and other tools.
On and around the benches are pieces of armor, swords,
cannons and small arms in various stages of
completion.

In front of the furnace stands an apparently giant,
muscular MAN, stripped to the waist. He is picking up
and throwing coal at a group of about fifty
leather-aproned, giant CYCLOPEAN MEN.

The CYCLOPES are parrying the "coal" missiles and
throwing them back at the muscular MAN. They all seem
very angry. The muscular MAN and the CYCLOPES are
shouting at each other.

                    VULCAN
                (throwing coal)
        Two and a half percent on the basic
        rate is my final offer!

                    CYCLOPES
        Five percent on the basic rate! ...
        And a separate agreement for overtime!
        ... Six percent! ... No deal without
        an agreement on early retirement! ...
        Ten percent! ...
        And new shift arrangements!
        Five percent or no increased
        production! ... Etc.

                                    (CONTINUED)

>               VULCAN
>            (hurling coal)
>       Two and a half percent! Take it or
>       leave it!

The fighting continues.

CUT TO:

THE BARON AND CO. as they fall from the open chimney
in the roof of Vulcan's chamber and crash to the
floor, making a crater in it.

ANGLE ON VULCAN and the CYCLOPES as they hear and see
the BARON and CO. land at the other end of the
chamber. They stop fighting.

ANGLE ON the BARON and CO.

>               SALLY
>           (opening tightly
>           clenched eyes.
>           Amazed)
>       I'm still in one piece ...
>           (trying arms and
>           legs)
>       I think.

>               BARON
>           (matter of fact)
>       I can't imagine why. Our descent into
>       what I take to be the volcano of Mount
>       Etna should have been slowed by a
>       rising cushion of warm air. But the
>       damned thing seems to have gone out.

>               BERTHOLD
>       Oh, no, not more giants!

CUT TO:

BERTHOLD'S P.O.V. of VULCAN and the CYCLOPES as they
approach threateningly. They are all wielding hammers
and pokers and lumps of metal, and look gigantic.

ANGLE ON the BARON and CO. as they watch the
approaching "giants."

(CONTINUED)

56 CONTINUED:

> BERTHOLD
> I've got nothing against giants
> personally ...

CUT TO:

THE BARON AND CO.'S P.O.V. of VULCAN and the CYCLOPS
as they get nearer and bigger.

ANGLE ON the BARON and CO. in their crater.

> BERTHOLD
> Some of my best friends are giants ...
> if only they weren't so big.

CUT TO:

THE BARON AND CO.'S P.O.V. of VULCAN and the CYCLOPES
as they stop a few yards away. They seem massive.

CUT TO:

A WIDE SHOT of the BARON and CO. confronted by VULCAN
and the CYCLOPES. We see that VULCAN and the CYCLOPES
are actually very small, and that the BARON, when he
climbs out of the crater, towers over them.

> VULCAN
> (suspiciously)
> Can I help you tiny mortals?

> BARON
> I sincerely hope so. I am Baron
> Munchausen — you may have heard of me
> ... My friends and I are looking for
> three men. One with exceptional
> eyesight, one with superb hearing and
> powerful lungs, and one who's
> extremely large and strong.

> VULCAN
> We're *all* extremely large and strong
> here. I'm Vulcan, the god. And these
> are my giant employees, the Cyclopes.
> (shouting violently
> at the CYCLOPES)
> Who are, even now, going back to
> work!!!

57 INT.     **VULCAN'S WORKSHOP AREA**

VULCAN conducts the BARON and CO. through his
workshop, past armor, swords, cannon.

>                    VULCAN
> I'm willing to supply arms and
> equipment to anybody that's prepared
> to pay the price. Greeks, Trojans,
> Romans, Huns ... It's not my fault if
> they're crazy enough to slaughter each
> other, is it?
>                (to CYCLOPES)
> You manky crew! Your go slows don't
> impress me! I'm God! I've got all the
> time in the universe, here! All the
> time, me!
>                (to BARON)
> In the old days the staff used to get
> paid, on the dot, every thousand
> years. This lot expect them every
> century! Agh! It's outrageous!

>                    BARON
>                (indicating an
>                impressive
>                rudimentary rocket)
> What is that?

>                    VULCAN
> This is our prototype ... RX, er,
> intercontinental, radar sneaky, multi
> war-headed, nuclear missile.

>                    BARON
>                (bemused)
> Ah ... What does it do?

>                    VULCAN
> Kills the enemy.

>                    BARON
>                (impressed)
> *All* the enemy?

>                    VULCAN
> Aye, all of them. And all their wives,
> and all their children, and all their
> sheep and cattle, and cats and dogs.
>                (MORE)

(CONTINUED)

                              VULCAN (CONT.)
                    *All* of them. All of them gone for
                    good.

                              SALLY
                    That's horrible.

                              VULCAN
                    Well, you see, the advantage is you
                    don't have to see a single one of them
                    die. You see, I just sit comfortably,
                    thousands of miles away from the
                    battlefield, and simply press the
                    button.

                              BERTHOLD
                    Well, where's the fun in that?

                              VULCAN
                    Oh, we cater for all sorts here. You'd
                    be surprised.

                              BARON
                    It'll never sell. It's unnatural. It's
                    unchivalrous.

                              VULCAN
                              (knowingly)
                    It'll sell all right. But it is a bit
                    before its time. It won't go into
                    production, that one, for another
                    couple of hundred years. Come and have
                    some fodder.

58  INT.    **VULCAN'S DINING ROOM**

    The BARON and CO. are sitting at a table with VULCAN.
    The table, chairs and all the room decorations are
    made of gold and encrusted with huge diamonds and
    other precious stones. Fabulous diamond chandeliers
    hang from the ceiling. The walls are mirrored. In one
    corner of the room is one cow. On the table are
    demi-tasse cups and a golden tea pot.

                              BARON
                              (sipping from cup)
                    Mmm. Delicious.

(CONTINUED)

                    VULCAN
                  (swigging)
    Aye, it's not a bad drop of tea as far
    as nectar of the Gods goes ... You can
    stay here for as long as you like ...
    It's nice to have fresh company for tea.

                    BARON
                  (reaching for the
                  teapot)
    Thank you. It'll be a pleasure.

                    SALLY
                  (for the BARON's
                  benefit)
    I'm sorry, but we have to go soon ...
    We're in a hurry.

The door of the dining room opens and ALBRECHT (played
by BILL) enters pushing a gold trolley loaded with
plates full of dainty cakes. He is dressed like a
cross between a maid and a butler and is old and
rather decrepit.

                    VULCAN
    Oh, here comes my midget man-servant
    with the petits fours.

                    BERTHOLD
    ALBRECHT!

                    BARON
    ALBRECHT!

                    ALBRECHT
                  (amazed)
    Baron! Berthold! What are you doing
    here?

                    BARON
    Looking for you.

                    ALBRECHT
                  (guiltily)
    I haven't got the treasure any more
    ... I've spent it. Er, I mean, I gave
    it all to charity.
                  (indicating the
                  jewel-encrusted
                  room)

                                        (CONTINUED)

                         BARON
          I don't want the treasure ...
          Albrecht, this is Sally ... Sally,
          Albrecht.

                         SALLY
                      (encouraged)
          Hello.

                         BARON
          I want you to come and help us fight
          the Turk again.

                         ALBRECHT
          Oh ... I couldn't do that. Not now ...
          Not since I found myself.

The BARON, SALLY and BERTHOLD exchange looks, ALBRECHT
begins to set out the plates of tiny cakes.

                         ALBRECHT
          No, not since I found myself. No. No,
          I really, no. I never really wanted to
          be big and strong and lug heavy things
          about ... No. I now know I want to be
          dainty ... and sensitive. They call me
          their midget down here ... I love it
          ... It's bliss.

ALBRECHT continues to unload the trolley.

                         BERTHOLD
                      (to the BARON)
          He's gone funny.

At this point, wind begins to swirl about them.
Celestial MUSIC starts and the light becomes even more
brilliant. As the music swells, a shell, accompanied by
CHERUBS, rises from a pool of water. The shell opens,
revealing a beautiful naked GIRL (played by ROSE)
standing exactly like Botticelli's Venus. HANDMAIDENS
appear, borne on the wind from somewhere in the room
and flutter around her with her robes ... and then are
gone ... along with the MUSIC, CHERUBS and wind.
VULCAN, the BARON and BERTHOLD spring to their feet.
VENUS is now dressed and seated in the great shell.

                         VENUS
                      (simply)
          Hello.

                                        (CONTINUED)

                    VULCAN
               (obviously besotted)
          Darling, dearest, this is Baron
          Munchausen and his friends, Sally and
          Berthold ...
                    (to the BARON and
                     CO.)
          This is Venus, the Goddess, and my
          wife.

                    BARON
               (gobsmacked)
          Madam ... I am overwhelmed ...

                    VULCAN
               (fumbling in the
                pocket of his apron)
          Oh ... oh ... My love ... my life ...
          the alpha and omega of my existence
          ... I've got something here for you.

     VULCAN takes a lump of coal from his pocket and
     proceeds to crush it with both hands. There is a flash
     of lightning from the coal, and VULCAN opens his dirty
     hands to reveal a large gleaming diamond.

                    VULCAN
               (giving the diamond
                to VENUS)
          There's a diamond for you, my
          precious.

     VENUS takes the diamond and pecks VULCAN on the cheek.

                    VENUS
          You're so sweet.
                    (giving the diamond
                     to a HANDMAIDEN)
          Another diamond.

                    BARON
               (mouth dry, knees
                trembling)
          Madam ... I am, alas, unable to offer
          you so splendid a gift ... But allow
          me to say ... that you excel in beauty
          even the magnificent Catherine the
          Great of Russia ...

                                        (CONTINUED)

                         BERTHOLD
          Here we go.

                         BARON
          ... whose hand in marriage I once had
          the honor of declining.

                         VENUS
                    (flirting heavily)
          Baron, you flatter me.

                         BARON
          Not one jot, Madam ... not one tittle.

                         VENUS
                    (seductively)
          What a handsome moustache ...

VENUS sways closer to the BARON who ineluctably
reciprocates. It looks like mad uncontrollable love at
first sight. VENUS takes the BARON by the arm and
begins to draw him away from the others.

                         VENUS
                    (to the BARON)
          Shall we dance?

The BARON and VENUS glide across the dining room, as
if borne on the wind. VENUS guides them towards a
door. As they go, a short burst of steam shoots from
one of VULCAN's ears, betraying his rising pressure.
Otherwise, he is trying hard to retain a smile and
remain calm and friendly. However, BERTHOLD sees the
steam and susses the situation. He and SALLY exchange
worried looks.

As the BARON and VENUS go through the door we hear the
sound of an orchestra striking up a waltz.

                         VULCAN
                    (with rictus smile,
                    to BERTHOLD and
                    SALLY)
          Come and see the ballroom.


59  INT.    **VULCAN'S BALLROOM**

ANGLE ON the BARON and VENUS who are dancing two feet
above the floor and gaining height. The ballroom is a

                                        (CONTINUED)

59 CONTINUED:

beautiful dome supported by columns — looking much
like a Greek temple — floating in the middle of a pool
of water. The pool is ringed with waterfalls and
cascades rising into the darkness of this subterranean
grotto. The interior of the dome is painted with a
beautiful Baroque sky and great crystal chandeliers
hang from it.

60  INT. ENTRANCE TO VULCAN'S BALLROOM

ANGLE ON VULCAN, SALLY, BERTHOLD and ALBRECHT as they
arrive at the door to the ballroom, and look in. On
seeing the BARON and VENUS dancing at their present
altitude, VULCAN's pressure clearly increases, and
jets of steam escape from both ears.

                    VULCAN
                (indicating
                ballroom, fighting
                rage)
          Nice, isn't it? ... We've just had it
          done.

61  INT.     VULCAN'S BALLROOM—VULCAN'S POINT OF VIEW

Of the BARON and VENUS as they sweep through the air
and continue to rise.

62  INT.     ENTRANCE TO VULCAN'S BALLROOM

ANGLE ON VULCAN and the others in the doorway as a
particularly strong jet of steam shoots up from under
VULCAN's collar.

                    BERTHOLD
                (to VULCAN, with
                forced jollity)
          I can dance! Here, watch this!

To SALLY's embarrassment, BERTHOLD removes a comb from
the hair of one of the HANDMAIDENS, takes a piece of
paper from one of the petits fours and begins to blow
on it, accompanying himself in an extraordinary sort
of silent tap routine in an attempt to distract
VULCAN.

VULCAN watches BERTHOLD's uncanny display with

                                        (CONTINUED)

fascination, as BERTHOLD lures him away from the
ballroom door. However, BERTHOLD doesn't have much
stamina, and he soon begins to flag.

> BERTHOLD
> (to SALLY, desperate
> for a rest)
> Sally! ... You can dance, can't you?

> SALLY
> (firmly)

No.

> BERTHOLD
> (knackered, but
> keeping going)

Thanks.

SALLY suddenly decides to take control of the
situation, and she marches into the ballroom.

## 63  INT.   VULCAN'S BALLROOM

ANGLE ON SALLY as she stomps into the ballroom. The
BARON and VENUS are now waltzing amongst the
chandeliers. Their heads are just below the Baroque
ceiling — gloriously painted with clouds and cherubs
— and they are gazing rapturously into each other's
eyes. SALLY runs around, keeping below them.

> SALLY
> (shouting up)
> Hey! ... Stop! ... Come down! ... Stop
> it! ... We've got to go!

The BARON and VENUS continue dancing, oblivious of
everything except each other. The BARON has become
perceptibly younger.

> SALLY
> We've got to get back and save the
> town! ... Please! ... Baron! ...

> BARON
> (looking down)
> Don't fret. The town is in no
> immediate danger.

64  EXT.    BESIEGED CITY

The town square where CITIZENS and SOLDIERS are
desperately trying to barricade the gates and prevent
them from being battered down by the TURKS.

65  INT.    VULCAN'S BALLROOM

SALLY looks with suspicion at the BARON. She is
unconvinced. The BARON and VENUS continue dancing but
move together and lock in a passionate embrace. The
sky is no longer a painting ... but real. This is the
final straw for SALLY, and she stops running below the
BARON and VENUS, stands for a moment glaring up at
them, and then stomps back into the dining room.

66  INT.    VULCAN'S DINING ROOM

ANGLE ON SALLY as she enters the dining room. BERTHOLD
is still doing his grotesque VULCAN-distracting dance,
but is within seconds of collapse.

                    SALLY
                 (to VULCAN)
        The Baron's kissing your wife!

BERTHOLD falls over in a lather of sweat, while VULCAN
changes color (as if hardening and tempering). Steam,
smoke and flames, shoot from the top of his head. He
storms into the ballroom.

67  INT.    VULCAN'S BALLROOM

The BARON and VENUS are dancing among the clouds. Two
winged CHERUBS fly around them, about to entwine them
with a long satin banner. The BARON (looking even
younger) is about to present VENUS with a paper rose,
when ...

                    VULCAN
                 (off camera)
              HARLOT! WHORE!

His roar shatters the scene. The clouds turn stormy.
One of the CHERUBS drops his end of the banner, which
falls towards VULCAN who stands far below them. VULCAN
grabs the end of the banner, violently wrenching the

                                        (CONTINUED)

90

BARON and VENUS (who are entwined by the material) out
of the sky.

> VULCAN
> That's enough of that.

Enraged he tries to disentangle the BARON and VENUS
from the banner.

> VULCAN
> You strumpet!

> VENUS
> (trying to calm him)
> Darling ...

> VULCAN
> Don't you "darling" me ... you hussy! ...
> (to the BARON)
> And as for you! ...

VULCAN holds the BARON above him with one hand as
BERTHOLD and ALBRECHT look on appalled.

> BERTHOLD
> (to ALBRECHT)
> Do something! Save him!

> ALBRECHT
> (dithering)
> Er ...

> VENUS
> Darling ... Please! ... Don't be
> jealous!

> VULCAN
> I'm not jealous!

> VENUS
> (teasing)
> You never let me have any friends.

BERTHOLD nudges ALBRECHT as VULCAN with the BARON held
above him storms out of the ballroom with VENUS in
pursuit.

> ALBRECHT
> (more dithering)
> Er ...

68 INT.     DINING ROOM

                          VULCAN
                I won't have you wiggling at
                philanderers! You floozy!

                          VENUS
                        (outraged)
                Floozy!?

                          BARON
                        (intervening)
                Sir, I assure you ...

                          VENUS
                Floozy! I'm a goddess! I can do what I
                like!

                          VULCAN
                And I'm *the* god! So shut up!

VULCAN charges out of the dining room with the BARON.
The others give chase.


69 INT.     A CORNER OF VULCAN'S WORKSHOP

ANGLE ON VULCAN as he arrives, carrying the BARON, at
the edge of a hole in the floor in a corner of his
workshop. VENUS, SALLY, BERTHOLD, and ALBRECHT are
seconds behind him. BERTHOLD pushes ALBRECHT forward.

                          BARON
                I must insist that the lady is
                blameless ...

                          VULCAN
                        (to the BARON)
                Ungrateful mortal! ...

                          ALBRECHT
                Er ... Sir ... Vulcan ... Excuse
                me ...

                          VULCAN
                        (to the BARON)
                You'll pay for this!!


                                              (CONTINUED)

> ALBRECHT
> (to VULCAN)
> Why don't we just all sit down quietly
> and ...

VULCAN heaves the BARON into the hole, the still-entangled banner streaming behind. As he does so, ALBRECHT reaches out and grabs for the end of the banner.

> ALBRECHT
> (reasonable)
> Now let's not be too
> hasty ... Ahhh!

The BARON's momentum carries ALBRECHT into the hole with him.

> SALLY
> (to VULCAN,
> horrified)
> What have you done to them?!

> VENUS
> (to VULCAN)
> You small-minded petit bourgeois ...

> VULCAN
> Shut up, you trollop!

> BERTHOLD
> What have you done to the Baron ...

> VULCAN
> You want the Baron? ... You can have
> the Baron!

VULCAN picks up SALLY and BERTHOLD and drops them down the hole. VULCAN and VENUS are left staring at each other.

> VENUS
> (seductively)
> Did you enjoy that? Did I ... excite
> you?

> VULCAN
> Yes ... Very much.

They embrace passionately. All the furnaces flare up in unison, and all the machinery starts up.

**70 INT.    FALLING THROUGH THE VORTEX INTO SOUTH SEAS**

ANGLE ON the BARON, SALLY, BERTHOLD and ALBRECHT as
they fall through the center of the world, passing
from dim light to bright light and back again.

**71 EXT.    UNDERWATER WORLD**

ANGLE ON the underside of an enormous underwater rock
overhang. From a crevice the BARON and CO. appear,
continuing their fall in this, now open and empty,
sub-aqueous world. It continues to get lighter as they
plummet. Suddenly BERTHOLD breaks through a shimmering
surface below him. PANIC! It's as if he has burst
through the bottom of the vast bubble that encloses
this watery world. His legs dangle in the void below
the water. Desperately he struggles to swim upwards
into the safety of the water. The others too are
struggling to avoid dropping into the void. The others
too are struggling to avoid dropping into the void.
BERTHOLD is exhausting himself in his struggle when a
fish swims nonchalantly by ... upside down. BERTHOLD
suddenly realizes their predicament ... turns over and
looks out of the water into the void. He can see the
others' legs and bums hanging out of the water as they
struggle ... He can also see the void is in fact the
sky. They have fallen through the world and are merely
upside down in the South Seas.

ANGLE ON the surface of the sea as the BARON and CO.
right themselves and break the surface, gasping for
air.

                    BERTHOLD
                (coming to a new
                 realization)
        Oh, damn! I can't swim!
                (he begins flailing
                 about madly)

                    SALLY
        What's happening!? ... You've got old
        again!

                    BARON
                (looking old again
                 and miserable,
                 holding the, now
                 (MORE)

                                    (CONTINUED)

71 CONTINUED:

> BARON (CONT.)
> wet, limp, rose,
> intended for Venus)
> Well, what do you expect? I've just
> been expelled from a state of bliss
> ... And it's all your fault ...

> SALLY
> (to the BARON)
> Where are we?
> (Pause. Splashing
> the BARON:)
> Answer me!!!

> BARON
> (glum)
> The most probable explanation, if
> you're not an incurable skeptic, is
> that we've fallen through the center
> of the world and come out on the
> opposite side ... Somewhere in the
> South Seas.

> SALLY
> (appalled)
> But that's miles away!

> BARON
> Oh, well done! It's as good a place to
> die as any.

> ALBRECHT
> (upset, floating)
> I was happy in my volcano! ...

> BARON
> So was I!

> BERTHOLD
> (paddling
> desperately)
> Anyone keen to win a medal for
> lifesaving?

> ALBRECHT
> Don't struggle. Float naturally.

>                    BERTHOLD
>                    (drowning)
>          I don't float naturally! I sink
>          naturally!

>                     SALLY
>          Look!

CUT TO:

SALLY'S P.O.V. of what appears, in the distance, to be
a long black island.

>                   SALLY (V.O.)
>          An island!

>                  ALBRECHT (V.O.)
>          Is there a volcano on it?

>                    BERTHOLD
>          Oh shut up about your poxy volcano!

We see a fountain of something shooting up into the
air form the middle of the island.

>                   SALLY (V.O.)
>                   (surprised)
>          I think there *is*  a volcano on it.

The island seems to grow and change shape.

>                   SALLY (V.O.)
>                  (shock horror)
>          It's moving!!!

As the island rises it seems to develop a huge pair of
eyes which emerge from under the sea.

ANGLE ON the BARON and CO.

>                    BERTHOLD
>                   (terrified)
>          I spy with my little eye something
>          beginning with "M."

>                    ALBRECHT
>                   (hysterical)
>          It's a demon of the deep!!!

(CONTINUED)

                        BERTHOLD
           That begins with a "D," you klutz!
           It's "M," for monster.

                        SALLY
           Will it eat us?

                        BARON
                    (low)
           With any luck.

Suddenly, with a rush of water, two vast pink fleshy
walls, lined with teeth, shoot up vertically on either
side of the BARON and CO. BERTHOLD, ALBRECHT and SALLY
shout and scream. They are completely engulfed. The
giant fish closes its mouth around them, continues
gracefully through the arch of its leap, and dives out
of sight.


72  **INT. IN THE STOMACH OF THE GIANT FISH**

ANGLE ON SALLY clinging to a spar of rotten wood in a
torrent of swirling water. The water level begins to
drop rapidly, leaving SALLY hanging onto what we now
see is the skeleton of a large shipwreck. The receding
water deposits the half-drowned BERTHOLD and ALBRECHT
in the wreckage, close to SALLY. High overhead is the
dripping vault of the fish's stomach. SALLY, finding
that BERTHOLD and ALBRECHT are safe, looks around for
the BARON. She sees him, hanging, inert, from a rotten
spar. He is still clutching the rose which he tried to
give to Venus.

SALLY, followed by ALBRECHT and BERTHOLD, scrambles
over the wreckage to the BARON.

                        ALBRECHT
           I think he's dead.

                        SALLY
                    (beside herself)
           He can't be dead!

The BARON gives a groan as ALBRECHT and BERTHOLD lift
him down to the base of the wreckage. SALLY is very
relieved.

                        ALBRECHT
           He's not very perky, is he?

                                        (CONTINUED)

                              BERTHOLD
                    Hm. Is there a doctor in the fish?

                              BARON
                              (mumbles)
                    No doctors ... no doctors ...

The BARON sniffs the rose and faints.

                              SALLY
                              (matronly)
                    We've got to get him warm and dry.

                              ALBRECHT
                              (looking around)
                    Maybe there's a volcano in here.

                              BERTHOLD
                    Good heavens! All these years and I
                    never knew the anatomy of fish was
                    your speciality.

                              SALLY
                              (pointing through
                              the gloom)
                    There's something glowing over there.

                                                        CUT TO:


SALLY'S P.O.V. where we see a large, dark, looming
shape in the middle distance. Near the top of the
shape is what appears to be a lit window.

ANGLE on the BARON and CO.

                              SALLY
          Come on.

ALBRECHT and BERTHOLD pick up the BARON and begin to
follow SALLY through knee-deep water towards the
light.

Approaching the dark shape, SALLY and CO. discover it
to be a heap of wrecked ships piled one on top of the
other. The ships at the bottom of the pile, which are
full of holes, are supported and kept upright by
wooden props. A huge, sinister, ship's figurehead
peers down at SALLY and CO. as they wind their way,
beneath the carcasses of the rotting ships to the
source of light, which is coming from windows high on

                                                  (CONTINUED)

the hull of an ancient galleon called the "Sargasso Sea."
They hear a distant dirge-like singing.

> SALLY
> (looking up at the
> lights and shouting)
> Hello!

Pause. The singing continues.

> BERTHOLD
> (shouting louder)
> Ahoy there!

Pause. The singing continues.

> ALBRECHT
> (nervous)
> I don't like this.

## 73 INT.    GIANT FISH — SHIP DECK

ANGLE ON SALLY followed by BERTHOLD and ALBRECHT
carrying the BARON, as they climb crude, rickety,
wooden steps onto the deck of the galleon. The deck is
strewn with broken rigging and ship's gear. They look
around for a moment before SALLY leads them towards a
smashed doorway leading into the poop.

> ALBRECHT
> (frightened)
> Don't go in there.

> SALLY
> (indicating the
> BARON)
> We need help.

SALLY continues through the doorway — the OTHERS follow.

## 74 INT.    GIANT FISH — INSIDE SHIP

SALLY and CO. enter a dark room from where a ladder
leads through a trap door to a cabin above which seems
to be where the light is coming from. SALLY and CO.
struggle up the ladder until, looking into the
illuminated cabin, they see the ship's CAPTAIN and a
group of SAILORS, slowly, lethargically, playing cards

(CONTINUED)

around a table. An OLD SAILOR is sitting in the corner with his hands cupped to his ears, singing the awful shanty dirge.

Throughout the action we hear:

> OLD SAILOR
> (singing)
> Oh once I had a sweetheart,
> A sweetheart once I had,
> She was the fairest beauty true,
> Her eyes were like the ocean blue,
> But her name was Davy Jones, O,
> Her name was Davy Jones.
>
> Oh once I had a sweetheart,
> A sweetheart once I had,
> She was the truest beauty fair,
> Gold was the color of her hair
> But her name was Davy Jones, O,
> Her name was Davy Jones.
>
> Oh once I had a sweetheart,
> A sweetheart once I had,
> She was the fairest true beau-ty,
> Her lips were red as red could be,
> But her name was Davy Jones, O,
> Her name was Davy Jones.
> (repeat ad nauseam)

SALLY enters the cabin, followed by BERTHOLD and ALBRECHT who are supporting a weak and despondent BARON.

The BARON is still clutching the rose which he attempted to give to VENUS.

> SALLY
> (nervously)
> Excuse me ... hello ... Excuse me ...
> We've just been swallowed, and ... we
> need some help ...

> BARON
> NO doctors ... no doctors.

> ADOLPHUS
> Do I hear the Baron?

(CONTINUED)

                         GUSTAVUS
          Eh?

                         ADOLPHUS
          I think it's the Baron.

                         GUSTAVUS
                     (looking at the
                      BARON)
          I think it's the Baron.

                         ADOLPHUS
          That's what I just said! Use your
          trumpet!

GUSTAVUS hits ADOLPHUS with his trumpet.

                         BARON
                     (moderately excited)
          Adolphus! Gustavus! Is it really you?

They all embrace.

                         ADOLPHUS
          So ... you're dead at last, eh?

                         GUSTAVUS
          We were beginning to think you might
          be immortal.

                         SALLY
          We're not dead.

                         BERTHOLD
          Sally, this is Adolphus, who used to
          be able to hit a bull's-eye halfway
          round the world. And Gustavus who
          could blow down a forest with one
          breath.

                         ADOLPHUS
          Those were the days, eh? When we were
          young and alive.

                         SALLY
                     (irritated)
          You're not dead!
                     (to BARON)
          But they're ever so old. Can they
                     (MORE)

                                        (CONTINUED)
                         101

                          SALLY (CONT.)
          really help?
                    (to ADOLPHUS)
          How do we get out of here?

                          ADOLPHUS
                    (puzzled)
          Out?

                          GUSTAVUS
                    (who's been using
                    his ear trumpet)
          You can't get out ... You're dead.

                          ALBRECHT
          How do you mean?

                          ADOLPHUS
          It's no good fighting it.

                          SALLY
          We're *not* dead!

                          GUSTAVUS
          We all die y'know ... You have to
          accept it ... We're all dead here ...
          This is hell.

                          ADOLPHUS
          Heaven.

                          GUSTAVUS
          Purgatory.

                          ADOLPHUS
          One of those places anyway.

                          SALLY
          Don't be stupid.

                          ADOLPHUS
                    (indicating empty
                    chairs)
          Sit down ... relax ... have a game ...
          You're dead for a long time.

The BARON sits down at the table. BERTHOLD and
ALBRECHT look at one another, shrug, and then follow
the BARON's example. SALLY watches this with dismay.

                                        (CONTINUED)
                          102

SALLY
What are you doing?

The BARON ignores SALLY. He is dealt a hand of cards
by the hooded skeletal figure of DEATH who is sitting
beside him but partially hidden by a broken beam.

SALLY
(angry)
You're giving up, aren't you?!

The BARON continues to ignore her.

SALLY
You can't give up! I won't let you!

BARON
(tetchily)
Go away! Clear off!

We see that DEATH has dealt the BARON a sinister hand.
The queen, jack, and ace of spades.

SALLY
What about Rose and Daisy and my
father and all the others?! You
promised to help them!

BARON
They're all perfectly safe!


75  EXT.    SQUARE

A quick scene of the town square where the gates look
as though they are about to give way under the
battering the TURKS are giving them. Smoke and flames
are everywhere and things look very bad.


76  INT.    GIANT FISH—INSIDE SHIP

BARON
They can look after themselves.
Besides ... there are more important
things.

SALLY
(furious)
Such as?

(CONTINUED)

> BARON
> (sniffing the limp
> rose)
Well ...

The BARON indicates to DEATH that he wants another
card. DEATH deals him a joker. At this point SALLY
recognizes DEATH, screams, and knocks all the cards
out of his hands.

> BARON
> (shouting angrily)
> You horrible little brat! Can't you
> let me die in peace once in a while!!!

From somewhere below decks, in the bowels of the ship,
we hear a strange whinnying-like sound. This is
followed by the noise of wild running feet which seem
to travel back and forth within the ship, all the time
getting close to the cabin. The GANG look at each
other in growing terror. The BARON puts SALLY down and
pushes her over to the GANG for protection. He draws
his saber and faces the door of the cabin in
preparation to do battle with the THING when it
arrives. The moment comes when the running feet seem
to be approaching the door of the cabin. The BARON and
CO. brace themselves for a terrifying encounter. Our
focus is on the door. Suddenly, the interior (of the
ship) wall of the cabin is being beaten in by some
tremendous force. Repeated blows are struck at it
until the wood begins to splinter and break. The BARON
and CO. retreat to the opposite side of the cabin and
take cover as best they can behind bits of furniture.
The blows to the wall of the cabin continue until a
section of it disintegrates leaving a large hole
through which steps an elderly, mangy-looking horse.

> BARON
> (overjoyed)
> Bucephalus! He must have heard me
> shouting!

The BARON embraces BUCEPHALUS.

> BARON
> Bucephalus! My Bucephalus!

BUCEPHALUS nuzzles the BARON. The GANG is relieved and
amazed. SALLY pats BUCEPHALUS.

(CONTINUED)

                              BARON
                    This is a good omen, what?

                            BERTHOLD
                            (doubtful)
                    Oh, yeah. Yeah.

                              BARON
                         (indicating door)
                    Prepare a rowing boat and be ready to
                    leave.

The GANG exchange puzzled looks. The BARON steps to the
cabin window and opens it. He takes a large container
of snuff from inside his jacket.

                              BARON
                    I have learned from experience that a
                    modicum of snuff can be most
                    efficacious.

The BARON opens the snuff-box and throws the contents
out of the window. He places one hand over his own nose
and one hand over BUCEPHALUS' nose.

## 77  EXT.    GIANT FISH

ANGLE ON the exterior of the GIANT FISH, as it begins
to vibrate and thrash about. Its eyes rotate.

## 78  INT.    GIANT FISH—INSIDE SHIP

ANGLE ON the interior of the cabin which is vibrating
and shaking. The GANG staggers towards the cabin door
and begins to exit.

## 79  INT.    GIANT FISH

ANGLE ON the interior of the fish as the stacks of
rotting ships begin to shake and crumble.

## 80  EXT.    GIANT FISH

ANGLE on the exterior of the GIANT FISH as it expels a
fountain of water and debris through its blowhole. Amongst
the debris is the rowing boat containing SALLY and CO.

81  **EXT.      SEASCAPE      DAY**

    ANGLE ON a mist-covered seascape as SALLY and CO. haul
    themselves back into their boat and bail it out.

                        BERTHOLD
                   (inhaling deeply)
            Fresh air! Ill never eat fish again
            ... if they promise not to eat me.

                          SALLY
            Where's the Baron?

    They look around for the BARON.

                          SALLY
            Baron!

    Silence.

                          SALLY
            Baron!

    SALLY looks at ALBRECHT and BERTHOLD, who avert their
    eyes. SALLY begins to cry. The others try to comfort
    her. At this moment a hand appears out of the water
    some distance form the boat. SALLY and CO. stare at it
    with bated breath. The hand reaches back into the
    water. It then re-emerges, lifting up the BARON by his
    pigtail. (It is in fact the BARON's own hand.) The
    BARON pulls himself and BUCEPHALUS, (restored to his
    prime) on whom he is still sitting, clear out of the
    water. SALLY and CO. look on, pleased but dumbfounded.

                          BARON
            Well, come one, I can't keep this up
            for ever!


82  **EXT.      SEASCAPE      DAY**

    ANGLE ON the rowing boat now containing the BARON,
    BUCEPHALUS, SALLY and CO. It moves through the mist,
    passing between the masts of sunken vessels. As the
    mist clears, the BARON and CO. see that they are back
    within sight of the town and TURKISH CAMP. The flag is
    still flying above the city walls.

                                              (CONTINUED)

> SALLY
> (amazed)
> Look! The town! We're here!

> BARON
> (rather smug)
> Yes. And the flag's still flying. I
> told you there was nothing to worry
> about.

There is a series of distant explosions and within
moments, cannon balls begin to land in the water all
around them.

**83  EXT.     TURKISH CANNON     DAY**

ANGLE ON the Turkish camp where TURKISH SOLDIERS are
re-positioning their cannons and firing them at the
BARON and CO.

**84  EXT.     ROWING BOAT AT SEA     DAY**

Cannonballs are still raining down around the boat.

> BERTHOLD
> Oh my gawd! The Sultan's army! Quick!
> Back in the fish!

> BARON
> (coolly)
> They are inviting us to defeat them.
> We must oblige.
> (he draws his saber)
> On a count of three: Gustavus — blow
> them back to Asia Minor. Adolphus —
> find the Sultan and shoot him!
> Albrecht — pull for the shore!
> Berthold — make yourself useful! One,
> two, three!

The GANG look at each other in impotent astonishment.

> BERTHOLD
> You couldn't make it "four," could
> you?

A cannonball tears through the boat which instantly
begins to sink.

(CONTINUED)

                          SALLY
          We're going down.

                          BARON
          Abandon ship!

                          BERTHOLD
          I think the ship's abandoning us,
          mate.

The boat sinks, depositing everyone in the water.

                          BERTHOLD
                       (frantic)
          I still can't swim!


85  EXT.    A ROCKY BEACH CLOSE TO THE TOWN      DAY

ANGLE ON the BARON and CO. as they struggle out of the
sea onto the rocky beach some distance from the town.
All around them are the sunken and washed up ships of
the town fleet. Beyond these wrecks, out at sea, are
the Turkish ships which are still firing at them.

                          BARON
                     (spitting sea water)
          This is absolutely dreadful ...

                          SALLY
          It's hopeless.

                          BARON
                     (lying on his back
                      to empty the water
                      from his boots)
          I've never before been in such a
          disastrous rout! ... I'm usually on
          the winning side!

                          ALBRECHT
          If you weren't so competitive you
          wouldn't get so upset.

                          BERTHOLD
          Albrecht's useless!
                     (to SALLY)
          I've been trying to tell him about my
          legs.

                                          (CONTINUED)

                    ADOLPHUS
                (dragging himself up
                the beach)
        Well, there's nothing wrong with us,
        is there, Gustavus?!

                    GUSTAVUS
                (removing a crab
                from his ear
                trumpet)
        Eh?

                    SALLY
        We might as well give up.

                    BARON
                (surprised)
        You mustn't say that. Not *you*.


**86  EXT.    SAND DUNES    DAY**

        BERTHOLD, ALBRECHT, GUSTAVUS and ADOLPHUS are lying
        exhausted on the ground as the BARON, watched by SALLY
        and BUCEPHALUS, draws a plan of action in the sand
        with his saber.

                    BARON
            Now, is we begin attacking from two
            directions simultaneously, we compound
            surprise with confusion. Albrecht and
            Gustavus will provide the major
            themes, as it were, to the battle,
            while Adolphus and Berthold ...

                    SALLY
        Baron.

                    BARON
        Don't interrupt ... What is it?

                    SALLY
        This isn't going to work.

                    BARON
                (irritated)
        What do you mean?


                                        (CONTINUED)

                    109

>                    SALLY
>               (indicating the
>               others who are flat
>               out)
>     They're all old and tired ... It's not
>     like it used to be ... Don't you see?

The BARON looks at the others.

BERTHOLD, ALBRECHT and ADOLPHUS raise their heads
slightly and look blankly at the BARON. For a moment
the BARON seems taken aback. He then drops his saber
in the sand and sets off out of the dune.

>                    SALLY
>     Where are you going?

>                    BARON
>     To give myself up.

>                    SALLY
>     What?

The BARON stops at the top of the dune and turns.

>                    BARON
>     I gave my word that I'd raise the
>     siege and save the town. And I
>     gathered you all together for that
>     purpose ...

The BARON looks around at the group. They all look
sheepish and uncomfortable under his gaze.

>                    BARON
>     If you wish to see Baron Munchausen
>     again ... You'll have to do something
>     about it.

The BARON turns and continues on his way. SALLY chases
him and catches up with him.

>                    SALLY
>     You can't give yourself up! They might
>     kill you! ...
>               (pause)
>     And then we'll have spent all that
>     time in that smelly fish for nothing!

(CONTINUED)

86  CONTINUED:

The BARON leaves SALLY and marches on towards the
Turkish camp.

87  **EXT.**    **TURKISH CAMP**    **DAY**

ANGLE ON the BARON striding confidently between the
Turkish tents. He salutes astonished TURKISH SOLDIERS
and doffs his hat to their female CAMP FOLLOWERS.

88  **EXT.**    **TURKISH CAMP**    **THE SULTAN'S TENT**    **DAY**

ANGLE ON the BARON as he approaches an impressive
tent. This is much larger than the other tents,
covered with colorful designs and pennants, and
surrounded by GUARDS. The BARON walks confidently past
the GUARDS, who are too amazed to challenge him, lifts
the flap of the tent, and enters.

89  **INT.**    **INSIDE THE SULTAN'S TENT**    **DAY**

The BARON steps into the SULTAN's tent. Here he finds
the SULTAN and JACKSON sitting drinking wine and
discussing business. The SULTAN's TIGER is lying on
the flower-strewn rug. JACKSON is wearing a disguise.
Neither of them notices the BARON.

                    JACKSON
                (consulting papers)
        So ... it's agreed ... on Friday the
        28th, you surrender. That's three
        weeks tomorrow. We can fix the details
        later.

                    SULTAN
        No, no, no. *You* surrender.

                    JACKSON
        With respect, Sultan, we've been
        through all this. *You* surrender.

                    SULTAN
        But we're winning.

                    JACKSON
        We surrendered last time.

(CONTINUED)

                          SULTAN
            So?

                          JACKSON
            So now it's your turn.

                          SULTAN
            I still don't get it.

                          JACKSON
            Listen, if we surrender again, that's
            twice in succession. It all becomes
            terribly lopsided. Unbalanced. Whereas
            if you surrender, it's symmetrical.

                          SULTAN
            What about the virgins?

                          JACKSON
            Please. Forget the virgins. We're out
            of virgins. Let us instead concentrate
            on reaching a rational, sensible, and
            civilized agreement which will
            guarantee a world fit for science,
            progress, and —

                          BARON
            But not Baron Munchausen.

    The SULTAN and JACKSON spring to their feet.

                          SULTAN
            Baron!

                          JACKSON
            You! The old lunatic!

                          BARON
                    (stepping forward)
            I'm afraid so.

                          SULTAN
            Guards! Help! Murder!

    Half a dozen GUARDS dive into the tent and grab the
    BARON.

                          SULTAN
            Who let this man into my tent?

                                        (CONTINUED)

The GUARDS shake their heads and look worried.

>                    BARON
>               (nonchalantly)
>          Sultan ... if you're still interested
>          in my head ... it's yours ... I'm
>          tired of it.

>                    SULTAN
>          Send for the executioner!

One of the GUARDS exits.

>                    BARON
>          So, Mr. Jackson, still the "rational"
>          man, eh? How many people have perished
>          in your logical little war?

>                    JACKSON
>          There are certain rules, sir, to the
>          proper conduct of living. We cannot
>          fly to the moon. We cannot defy death.
>          We must face the fact ... no, the
>          folly of fantasists like you, who
>          don't live in the *real* world ... and
>          who consequently come to a very sticky
>          end.

>                    SULTAN
>               (offering a glass of
>               wine to the BARON)
>          A last drink, Baron? Excellent Tokay.

**90  EXT.      THE TURKISH CAMP      EXECUTION SITE      DAY**

ANGLE ON a prayer crier standing in the tower.

ANGLE ON the BARON standing on a raised platform
outside the Sultan's tent. On the platform, beside the
BARON, holding a scimitar, is the EXECUTIONER. The
platform is surrounded by a large audience of Turkish
SOLDIERS. In front of these, in the best seats, are
the SULTAN and JACKSON (in disguise). Beside the
platform, a DRUMMER is beating a slowly quickening
rhythm.

>                    SULTAN
>               (to the BARON)
>          Have you any famous last words?

>                                        (CONTINUED)

                         BARON
                    (cooly)
          Not yet.

                         SULTAN
                    (puzzled)
          "Not yet"?
                    (to JACKSON)
          Is that famous?

                         JACKSON
                    (shaking his head)
          The man's a buffoon.

                              SULTAN
          Executioner!

The EXECUTIONER steps forward.

                              SULTAN
          Execute!

The BARON, obligingly, kneels down and cranes his neck
forward. The dotted line is printed around his neck.
The pace and volume of the drumming increases. The
blind EXECUTIONER raises his scimitar. The ODALISQUES
in their cages anxiously watch the scene. The
EXECUTIONER is on the point of bringing it down to a
crescendo of drumming, when "PING," something strikes
the weapon, knocking it from his hand, sending it
spinning directly at the SULTAN, slicing through his
turban and barely missing his skull.


91  **EXT.**     **A DISTANT SAND DUNE**     **DAY**

ANGLE ON ADOLPHUS, as he lowers the BARON's still
smoking musket from his shoulder and peers in the
direction in which he has just shot. With him on the
sand dune are SALLY and BERTHOLD.

                         SALLY
                    (leaping up and down
                     excitedly)
          You did it!


92  **EXT.**     **THE TURKISH CAMP**     **EXECUTION SITE**     **DAY**

ANGLE ON THE BARON, at the execution site, as

                                        (CONTINUED)

BUCEPHALUS, the BARON's saber on his back, jumps over
the AUDIENCE and gallops past the execution platform.
The BARON vaults onto BUCEPHALUS, scattering the
AUDIENCE in confusion.

                                                    CUT TO:

THE SULTAN as he shouts to his GENERALS who start to
rise from their seats, but before they reach standing
position the BARON charges down the line lopping their
heads neatly off with his saber. The BARON glances
back at them, and WE SEE a row of headless bodies fall
over. The SULTAN stands frozen as the BARON charges
towards him, saber swinging down. But rather than
slicing through another neck the BARON slices the tent
pole and the SULTAN and JACKSON are engulfed by the
collapsing canopy of the pavilion and trapped with the
TIGER. The BARON waves his sword toward his distant
GANG.

                          BARON
          I knew we could do it! All together
          now!

93  EXT.     A DISTANT SAND DUNE     DAY

ANGLE ON GUSTAVUS on another sand dune. He takes an
enormously deep breath and exhales violently towards
the Turkish camp. Throughout this battle sequence,
BERTHOLD, ALBRECHT, ADOLPHUS and GUSTAVUS remain old
men, and never quite return to their "Sultan's Tale"
form. They succeed, by dint of making enormous
efforts, in producing enough of their youthful talents
and vigor to be extremely effective.

94  EXT.     THE TURKISH CAMP     DAY

ANGLE ON THE TURKISH CAMP as a violent wind
(fluctuating in the pattern of GUSTAVUS' breathing)
whips up clouds of dust and flattens tents. TURKISH
SOLDIERS are panicking and running everywhere. The
TURKISH CAVALRY struggle in the wind. An ELEPHANT is
blown onto a rock and the tower on its back
disintegrates. The other elephants are led back to
their compound. A group of soldiers runs and a tent
blows into them.

GUSTAVUS starts to pant. A TURKISH CAVALRYMAN sees the
BARON fighting another MOUNTED TURK and mounts his

                                              (CONTINUED)
                          115

horse. He charges up towards the BARON, his lance at
the ready. As the BARON knocks the MOUNTED TURK from
his horse, he is just about to deal the BARON a fatal
blow, when he is hit by something unseen and falls to
the ground. The BARON turns to stare at him.

95 **EXT.**     **A DISTANT SAND DUNE**     **DAY**

ANGLE ON ADOLPHUS as he lowers his smoking musket to
reload. Nearby GUSTAVUS begins hacking and wheezing,
trying to get his breath. SALLY tries thumping him on
the back. The wind stops for a moment. He finally
responds to SALLY's thumping and with a mighty gasp,
begins to inhale. Air, leaves and dust roar into his
open mouth.

96 **EXT.**     **THE TURKISH CAMP**     **DAY**

Still unseen by the BARON, the CAVALRYMAN swings his
sword downwards. But just before the blade slices
through the BARON, BERTHOLD screeches in with a
Turkish shield. CLANG! The blade strikes the shield.
The CAVALRYMAN drops his sword as it rings and
vibrates out of control. The noise makes the BARON
turn and he runs the CAVALRYMAN through. The body
crashes to the ground. The BARON looks down to see
BERTHOLD for the first time — lying under the corpse —
gasping for breath.

> BARON
> This is no time for napping, we're
> fighting a battle.

97 **EXT.**     **DISTANT SAND DUNE**     **DAY**

GUSTAVUS finally responds to SALLY's thumpings and,
with a mighty gasp, begins to inhale. Air, leaves,
dust roar into his open mouth.

98 **EXT.**     **TURKISH CAMP**     **DAY**

Tents are being sucked from their guy ropes. SOLDIERS,
equipment begin to slip and slide towards the distant
GUSTAVUS and SALLY.

**99 EXT.     DISTANT SAND DUNE     DAY**

Despite their struggling, TURKISH SOLDIERS are being
sucked up the sand dune towards GUSTAVUS' open maw.
Then the moving air stops again. GUSTAVUS' lungs can
hold no more. His mouth is stuffed with twigs and
leaves. Once again he is gagging. SALLY is terrified.
The TURKISH SOLDIERS have recovered from their slide,
are getting to their feet, spears at the ready, and
are almost upon GUSTAVUS and SALLY. She is banging
madly on his back, trying to dislodge the blockage in
his throat. Just as the spears reach them — GAAGH!! —
GUSTAVUS exhales. The SOLDIERS are blown high in the
air.

**100 EXT.     TURKISH CAMP     DAY**

The SULTAN and JACKSON have managed to disentangle
themselves form the collapsed pavilion. JACKSON pulls
his cloak over his face and scuttles away. The SULTAN,
half out from under the tent, starts to shout orders
when he looks up. Hurtling down from the sky are
several spear-carrying SOLDIERS. The SULTAN dives
under the canvas just as the spears thud around him,
SOLDIERS crashing everywhere.

                                                    CUT TO:

THE BARON, who spots JACKSON escaping. He turns to
Pursue him but his path is blocked by a platoon of
TURKISH PIKEMEN. As he deals with them a SNIPER on top
of an elephant-back tower takes aim.

**101 EXT.     DISTANT SAND DUNE     DAY**

ANGLE ON ADOLPHUS and BERTHOLD on the dune. ADOLPHUS
pulls the trigger of his musket. The musket, however,
fails to fire. Frantically he shouts to BERTHOLD,
indicating the SNIPER.

**102 EXT.     TURKISH CAMP     DAY**

BERTHOLD races off in a cloud of dust. As he runs, he
trips on a lump of rock and crashes down the side of
some rocks, landing with a WALLOP. Hurriedly, he gets
up and whooshes off towards the camp. WE SEE the BARON
fighting through the line of PIKEMEN as BERTHOLD races
past in the distance towards the tower. But before he

                                          (CONTINUED)

reaches it, the SNIPER fires. BERTHOLD screeches to a halt. The bullet whistles past with BERTHOLD in pursuit. He catches it up, grabs it, but OW!!—it's red hot and he lets it go. The bullet continues on its way. BERTHOLD accelerates past it.

NEW ANGLE ON BERTHOLD whooshing into SHOT, grabbing a discarded piece of elbow armor and raising it just in time to deflect the bullet from the BARON's back. The bullet strikes the tip of a spear about to impale the BARON, shattering it, then ricochets off and hits another spear intent on the same evil deed. CRACK! ZING! The spear is deflected the the bullet shoots off in another direction — towards BERTHOLD, who ducks just in time — flies back across the camp and ... hits the SNIPER square in the chest. As he falls form the tower, his foot catches in the rope attached to the camp's flag, and it shoots to the top of the flagpole.

BERTHOLD collapses. The BARON looks around and sees only BERTHOLD, slumped on the ground.

>                    BARON
>      Dammit, man, make yourself useful. I
>      can't do everything.

**103 EXT.    TURKISH CAMP    DAY**

A line of TURKISH CAVALRYMEN charge towards CAMERA in a row. The BARON turns and sees them and dashes off towards the SULTAN's tent. The CAVALRYMEN race after him. He races around the tent catching up with the end of the line of TURKISH CAVALRYMEN. He turns in on them, racing through shot in the same direction. The TURKS immediately follow behind him, forming a second parallel line of CAVALRYMEN. Almost as soon as the BARON leaves frame, he appears again from the other side of frame but closer to camera, and races through shot pursued by TURKISH CAVALRYMEN. Now there are three parallel lines of RACING HORSEMEN. Again, the moment after he leaves frame, the BARON appears from the opposite side pursued by TURKS. Now there are four lines. And once more he leaves frame only to appear again closer to camera with the TURKS in pursuit. We CUT TO a wide shot to reveal that the BARON has managed to get the TURKS racing around in an ever-decreasing spiral. Cutting to the center of the spiral, BUCEPHALUS with the BARON on his back, is standing on his hind legs spinning like a top.

104 **EXT.**     **DISTANT SAND DUNE**     **DAY**

GUSTAVUS has recovered.

> SALLY
> Now ... easy breaths, this time.

105 **EXT.**     **TOP OF ROCK**     **DAY**

ADOLPHUS fires his musket.

106 **EXT.**     **TURKISH CAMP**     **DAY**

ANGLE ON the Turkish Camp as the bullet hits a soldier
who falls forwards onto his gun, causing it to fire.
The bullet of his gun hits a powder keg sitting next
to a pile of cannonballs, which are blown up into the
air.

107 **EXT.**     **DISTANT SAND DUNE/TOP OF ROCK**     **DAY**

ANGLE ON SALLY AND GUSTAVUS on their sand dune as
cannonballs explode around them

ANGLE ON ADOLPHUS, also ducking from the explosions.

108 **EXT.**     **TURKISH CAMP**     **DAY**

ANGLE ON the Turkish cannons continuing to fire on the
gang.

109 **EXT.**     **DISTANT SAND DUNE**     **DAY**

TO SALLY AND GUSTAVUS

> SALLY
> Where's Albrecht?

110 **EXT.**     **PART OF HARBOR**     **DAY**

From the water lapping the rocks, ringing the harbor,
ALBRECHT appears. Over his shoulders are the anchors
of some sunken ships. The chains drag behind.

111  **EXT.**     **PART OF HARBOR**     **DAY**

ALBRECHT is pulling the anchor chains, swinging the ships.

112  **EXT.**     **TURKISH CAMP**     **DAY**

The Turkish camp is being blown to pieces by their own cannons. A cannonball hits the powder store near the land-based cannon, setting off a chain of devastating explosion. The cannons are destroyed.

All of these explosions are making the elephants in their compound very twitchy.

113  **EXT.**     **DISTANT SAND DUNE**     **DAY**

SALLY is holding a mouse by the tail.

> SALLY
> (to GUSTAVUS)
> Gently, this time.

GUSTAVUS blows, the mouse flies off.

114  **EXT.**     **TURKISH CAMP**     **DAY**

The mouse, now rolled up like a ball, bounces across the ground until it comes to rest amongst the elephants' feet. It unrolls itself and starts to run around. PANIC! The elephants go crazy. They stampede. The towers on their backs crash to the ground as they thunder off. The TURKISH TROOPS also panic as they see the elephants charging towards them. A mass stampede is underway.

> CUT TO:

THE SULTAN'S PAVILION. The SULTAN is just managing to cut his way through the pinned-down pile of canvas and escape, when the elephant stampede reaches him. Somehow the pounding feet miss him as he cowers under the canvas, but a trailing harness snags on the tent ropes and the pile of material, including the SULTAN, is swept up in the great ball and dragged, bouncing and banging, behind the elephants as they charge pell-mell into the audience.

> (CONTINUED)

120

CUT TO:

THE BARON, who is dealing with a few of the most desperate and hardened JANISSERIES, when a strange, ominous, whooshing noise is heard. The JANISSERIES look up.

CUT TO:

A GROUP OF RETREATING CAVALRYMEN who also look up towards the source of the noise. The retreating FOOTSOLDIERS increase their speed as they, too, take in the cause of the noise.

115 EXT.     TURKISH CAMP — SKY     DAY

ANGLE ON the sky where first one, then two, then three sunken ships fly into view — being swung in a giant arc.

116 EXT.     PART OF HARBOR     DAY

ANGLE ON ALBRECHT on a rock in the harbor — the anchor chains held tight in his hands as he spins round and round like a hammer thrower.

117 EXT.     TURKISH CAMP/PART OF HARBOR     DAY

Round and round swing the sunken ships. The TURKS are running for their lives.

ALBRECHT strains with the effort and then, with a mighty heave, he lets the chains go.

The ships hurtle through the air, flying high over the BARON as he watches them pass.

ALBRECHT falls backwards into the water.

118 EXT.     TURKISH CAMP     DAY

ANGLE ON TURKISH TROOPS racing away as the ships loom overhead. And then, with an earth-shaking crash, the ships smash into the ground, scattering the remains of the TURKISH ARMY.

**119 EXT.      PLAIN OUTSIDE THE TOWN      DAY**

ANGLE ON the TURKISH ARMY as it retreats into the
distance in a cloud of dust.

**120 EXT.      BATTLEMENTS OF RELIEVED TOWN — BARON'S P.O.V.**

Of the TOWNSPEOPLE and SOLDIERS on the battlements.
The CAMERA PANS along the cheering, waving CROWD until
it reaches one particular gap in the crenelations
where it stops on the face of a very unhappy-looking
HORATIO JACKSON.

**121 EXT.      IN WRECKAGE OF TURKISH CAMP      DAY**

The BARON, BUCEPHALUS, SALLY, ALBRECHT, BERTHOLD,
GUSTAVUS and ADOLPHUS, tired but triumphant, meet in
the wreckage of the TURKISH camp. The BARON's sword
arm thrashes around automatically from time to time.
They look towards the retreating Turks.

                         BERTHOLD
                        (dawning
                       realization)
              We did it! We DID IT!!!

BERTHOLD, SALLY, ALBRECHT, GUSTAVUS, ADOLPHUS and
BUCEPHALUS dance around, hugging each other. The BARON
looks on approvingly.

                         GUSTAVUS
              We've won!!!

                         ADOLPHUS
              We beat them! We've done it!

                         ALBRECHT
              YAHOO!!!

                         SALLY
              YIPPEE! They've gone!

                         ADOLPHUS
              Good riddance!
                        (shouting in the
                        wrong direction)
              And don't come back!!!

                                          (CONTINUED)

                            122

>               SALLY
>            (to the BARON)
>     We've won!
>
>               BARON
>     Of course.
>
>               BERTHOLD
>     WE DID IT!
>            (another kind of
>            dawning realization)
>     We did it?

GUSTAVUS and CO. stop cheering and dancing, and join
BERTHOLD in sober reflection.

>               GUSTAVUS
>            (doubtfully)
>     We've won?
>
>               ADOLPHUS
>     How the hell did we manage that?
>
>               ALBRECHT
>            (sinking, exhausted,
>            to the ground)
>     With considerable reluctance.

BERTHOLD and CO. collapse, joining ALBRECHT moaning on
the ground.


**122 EXT.    INSIDE THE GATES OF THE RELIEVED TOWN    DAY**

Cymbals crash, trumpets blare as the band strikes up
and the triumphal procession begins. The BARON, with
SALLY sitting in front of him on BUCEPHALUS, leads the
victorious GANG through the crowd-lined streets. From
her vantage place SALLY can see a banner raised above
the CROWE, on which is written (clearly hurriedly),
"HENRY SALT AND DAUGHTER PLAYERS." SALLY looks beneath
the banner where she sees SALT surrounded by the
THEATER PEOPLE. SALT smiles and waves at her. SALLY
smiles and waves back. (Obviously Sally's relationship
with her Dad has taken a turn for the better.) The
BARON and CO. continue on through the CROWD into the
town square where a giant bronze head of the BARON is
being reinstated on the damaged equestrian statue
which dominates the square.

## 123 EXT.     TOWN SQUARE     DAY

A TOP SHOT of the procession. A large stone wing is
revealed as the CAMERA moves. It hovers menacingly
over the square. A hand steadies itself on the wing.

## 124 EXT.     CATHEDRAL DOME     DAY

ANGLE ON a great stone gargoyle of death — wings
spread, scythe in one hand — jutting from the cornice
of the shattered dome of the cathedral. Leaning on its
back is JACKSON, carrying a musket. Clearly preparing
to use it, he takes aim.

## 125 EXT.     HIGH ABOVE THE TOWN SQUARE — JACKSON'S P.O.V.

As he lines up the sights of the musket on the BARON.
It is clear from this that SALLY is in danger too.

## 126 EXT.     TOWN SQUARE     DAY

ANGLE ON the BARON and CO. happily surrounded by
euphoric TOWNSPEOPLE. ROSE, DAISY and VIOLET plus
BABY, unable to reach him through the throng. He
laughs, doffs his hat and blows kisses to the
ACTRESSES. ARGUS leaps out from the crowds, welcoming
him.

## 127 EXT.     CATHEDRAL DOME     DAY

ANGLE ON HORATIO JACKSON as he pulls the trigger and
fires his musket.

## 128 EXT.     TOWN SQUARE     DAY

ANGLE ON the BARON as he is struck by JACKSON's
bullet. He jerks back, and topples from BUCEPHALUS.
SALLY is unaware of what has happened behind her.

For a second there is a terrible silence, before the
TOWNSPEOPLE, suspecting a sniper, become hysterical
and stampede all over the place, trampling on each
other as they go. BERTHOLD, ALBRECHT, ADOLPHUS and
GUSTAVUS run forward to tend to the BARON. SALLY
remains, stunned, on the back of BUCEPHALUS.

(CONTINUED)

124

                              BERTHOLD
            He's dying!


129  **EXT.**      **CATHEDRAL DOME**      **DAY**

     ANGLE ON the stone gargoyle as it moves. Cracking and
     tearing, it transforms itself into the living figure
     of DEATH, and ripping itself loose form the Cathedral,
     flies off leaving JACKSON momentarily exposed.
     Recovering from his shock at the moving gargoyle, he
     ducks down out of sight as someone shouts from below.

                         FROM BELOW (V.O.)
            There he is!


130  **EXT.**      **TOWN SQUARE**      **DAY**

     SOLDIERS begin firing up at the Cathedral roof. The
     GROUP around the BARON are in a desperate state.

                              DAISY
            Fetch a doctor! Hurry!

                              VIOLET
            Don't leave me, Baron, please don't
            leave me!

                              ROSE
            Get back! Give him air!

                              DAISY
                         (to SALT, concerned
                          for SALLY)
            Mind Sally.

     A BLACK FIGURE makes his way out of the panicking
     crowd towards the BARON.

                         PERSON IN CROWD
            Here's the doctor!

                              BARON
                         (barely alive)
            No ... no doctor.

     The DOCTOR leans over the BARON. SALLY is being pulled
     away and comforted by SALT. Suddenly ARGUS growls.
     SALLY turns back. The black-robed DOCTOR has changed

                                        (CONTINUED)

                         125

into the black-winged figure of DEATH. The others
don't seem to notice. SALLY breaks away form SALT and
begins attacking DEATH.

> SALLY
> NO! ... NO! ... GET AWAY! ... NO! ...
> LEAVE HIM ALONE! ... STOP! ... GO
> AWAY! ... STOP! ...
> > (etc.)

DEATH seems totally impervious to this attack. The
shaken SALT steps forward and tries to calm SALLY but
she fights him off.

> SALT
> Sally! What is it?!
> > (to ROSE, VIOLET and
> > DAISY)
> Quick! ... Help me! ... She's having a
> fit!

SALT, ROSE, VIOLET plus BABY and DAISY drag the
screaming, kicking, foaming at the mouth SALLY away
from the fallen BARON and the hooded figure of DEATH,
who has just managed to extract a glowing, fluttering
"thing" from out of the BARON's mouth.

> ROSE
> He's dead.

DEATH then turns and moves quickly away.

ARGUS follows him, snapping at his heels, and causes
him to trip. DEATH falls to the ground, and in so
doing, lets go of the fluttering and glowing thing
which he extracted from the BARON's mouth. This
"thing" flutters away and flies up above the town and
seems to dissolve into the sun.

131 EXT.      TOWN SQUARE      DAY

The great equestrian statue of the BARON and
BUCEPHALUS is draped in black crepe. At the base of
the statue a solemn procession is in progress. The
grief-stricken TOWNSPEOPLE line the street as the
BARON's funeral cortege makes its way towards a grave
that has been dug beneath the statue. SALLY is
inconsolable, the THEATER PEOPLE are in shock. The
GANG are old and defeated once again. As the PRIEST

(CONTINUED)

conducts the burial service, the glass-topped coffin
with the BARON's body is slowly lowered into the
grave. As the shadow of the grave passes over the
BARON's young, sublime face, we hear a VOICE OVER:

> BARON (V.O.)
> ... and that was only one of the
> several occasions on which I met my
> death ... an interesting experience
> which I don't hesitate strongly to
> recommend. And so, with the help of my
> inestimable servants, I defeated the
> Turks and saved the day. And from that
> time forth, everyone with a talent for
> it lived happily ever after.

## 132 INT.     THEATER STAGE     DAY

ANGLE ON BARON's face now old and withered as we first
saw him. He is standing on the stage of the theater.
The AUDIENCE is still there.

Behind him is the "underwear" balloon with its
galleon, suspended by wires from the top of the
proscenium arch. The bombardment has stopped but all
around are damaged buildings and injured people.

SALT, deeply moved, begins to applaud the BARON. He is
suddenly interrupted by the voice of HORATIO JACKSON.

> JACKSON (V.O.)
> Stop this nonsense at once!

## 133 INT.     THEATER STAGE     DAY

ANGLE ON HORATIO JACKSON arriving with ENTOURAGE and
SOLDIERS. The small manic DRUMMER BOY is still with
him.

> JACKSON
> You, sir, are under arrest for
> spreading ridiculous tales at a time
> of great danger ... when the enemy is
> at the gates! Arrest him!

The group of SOLDIERS standing close to JACKSON look
uneasy, but don't move.

(CONTINUED)

> JACKSON
> I order you to arrest that man!

The SOLDIERS move a couple of inches and stop.


**134 INT.     FRONT OF THEATER (TOWN SQUARE)     DAY**

A wide shot of the front of the theater as JACKSON begins to lose his cool.

> JACKSON
> Am I or am I not the elected
> representative?! Arrest him!

Nobody moves except the BARON, who jumps calmly down from the stage and, followed by ARGUS, walks through the AUDIENCE towards the hole in the wall.

> BARON
> (shouting out across
> the square)
> Open the gates!


**135 EXT.     FRONT OF THE THEATER     DAY**

ANGLE ON JACKSON and CO. on the forestage of the theater.

> JACKSON
> Do *not* open the gates! The Turks are
> outside, and we are not about to
> surrender!


**136 EXT.     TOWN SQUARE     DAY**

ANGLE ON the BARON and ARGUS as they leave the theater and stride across the square in the direction of the gates.

> BARON
> Open the gates! Open the gates!

SALT, stirred by the BARON's example, turns to his COMPANY.


(CONTINUED)

                        SALT
                    (heroically)
        Come on!


SALT, with RUPERT, BILL, JEREMY, and DESMOND, ROSE,
DAISY, VIOLET and whoever plays the SULTAN, follow the
BARON out of the theater and across the square. The
rest of the AUDIENCE exhange looks and then follow
SALT and the THEATER COMPANY. JACKSON is frantic. He
can't believe what's happening. He chases after the
AUDIENCE.

                      JACKSON
        Come back! I'm warning you! Anybody
        who opens those gates will be guilty
        of treason! ... Arrest that man! ...
        Now! ... This instant! ... Anyone who
        fails to arrest him is under arrest!
        ... And anyone who doesn't arrest them
        is under arrest! ... We will not
        tolerate a breakdown of law and order
        at this crucial moment in our history!
        ...

JACKSON runs at the back of the CROWD, but nobody
takes any notice of him, except for a group of thin,
cheeky KIDS who begin to gather around him. JACKSON,
thinking that he can head off the CROWD, dives into a
side street. The KIDS follow.


137 EXT.     **NEAR THE GATE**     DAY

        As the BARON and ARGUS with SALT, the THEATER COMPANY
        and the AUDIENCE from the theater, approach the
        barricaded gates, JACKSON with a COMPANY OF SOLDIERS
        run out of a side street and place themselves between
        the gates and the BARON.

                      JACKSON
                    (triumphant)
        The gates will remain closed.

        EVERYONE looks to the BARON. However, the BARON has
        been exhausted by telling his story and marching to
        the gates.


                                            (CONTINUED)

>                     BARON
>               (trying to shout but
>               only managing to
>               whisper)
>           Open the gates!

SALLY looks with concern at the flagging BARON. She
catches SALT's eye.

>                     SALT
>               (removing wig)
>           Open the gates!

>                     JACKSON
>               (to the SOLDIERS)
>           Shoot anyone who disobeys my orders.

>                     SALT
>               (moving forward)
>           Open the gates, dear friends, and
>           seize the day. Or close our minds up
>           with invention's death. In fear
>           there's nothing so destroys a man as
>           ignorant dullness and conformity. So
>           when the blast of hopelessness blows
>           in our ears, then imitate the actions
>           of the poet. Flex the mind's eye,
>           conjure up the brain, disguise
>           brutality with sympathetic urge.

SALT and the COMPANY have begun to press through the
tents of the amazed SOLDIERS. Some of thse hit out
half-heartedly at the THEATER COMPANY but are easily
overwhelmed.

>                     JACKSON
>               (apoplectic)
>           Shoot them! Stop them!

>                     SALT
>           On, on you noblest actors whose spirit
>           springs divine from ancient temples.
>           Grasp the mantle of the imagination,
>           leap the void, and perform the kind of
>           deed which might one day save the
>           world! Open the gates!

SALT and the THEATER COMPANY, plus the BARON, SALLY,
SOLDIERS and THEATER AUDIENCE remove the last bits of
barricade around the gate.

(CONTINUED)

                    JACKSON
          Stop! Have I not made myself clear?!!!
          I'll give you one more chance! Shoot
          these people at once! ... So it's
          treason then? ... Treason!

JACKSON has clearly gone doolally. The KIDS reappear
and laugh and dance around him. He strikes at them but
they dodge easily out of the way.

                    JACKSON
          You're under arrest! All of you! I
          want to see you all outside my office
          at four o'clock, when the bell
          tolls!!!

At this point, the gates are opened and JACKSON is
drowned out by the cheering of the THEATER COMPANY and
AUDIENCE. SALT and the THEATER COMPANY lift the BARON
and SALLY shoulder high and carry them out through the
gates.


138  THE GATES     DAY

The massive gates are swung open and the BARON is
carried through them followed by the THEATER COMPANY
and TOWNSPEOPLE. They look around and see bits of
abandoned Turkish siege equipment, battering rams,
guns, ammunition, broken tents, etc. Evidence that the
Turks have indeed been here, but no sign of the Turks
themselves. The TOWNSPEOPLE begin to shout and cheer.

                    TOWNSPEOPLE
          It's true! They've gone! The Turks
          have gone! He's beaten them! He's
          chased off the Turks! Three cheers for
          the Baron!
               (etc.)

As they cheer, a speck of dust appears in the
distance. It gets closer and closer until we see that
it's BUCEPHALUS, in his prime. He gallops up to the
BARON. The BARON mounts him. As he looks down at the
cheering TOWNSPEOPLE the BARON sees SALLY and the
THEATER PEOPLE push their way to the front of the
crowd. He takes the faded, water-logged rose meant for
Venus from inside his jacket, looks at ROSE with a
wistful expression, hesitates and, instead, turns and
gives it to SALLY.

                                        (CONTINUED)

> SALLY
> (to the BARON)
> It wasn't just a story, was it?

> BARON
> (with a twinkle in
> his eye, doffs his
> hat to SALLY)

The cheering CROWD now parts to let the BARON through
as he turns BUCEPHALUS and rides away towards the open
plain with ARGUS trotting by his side. He stops once
and turns to wave back at the PEOPLE at the gate. SALT
is standing with his arm around SALLY. And we, the
cinema audience, watch as the MUSIC swells and the
BARON rides off into the sunset.

The following sequences do not appear in the final shooting script or the finished film. They were excised from early drafts of the screenplay due to budgeting and scheduling considerations.

**This scene was to have opened the film, preceeding the credits:**

The screen is filled with an 18th Century mechanical
model of the solar system. The clockwork mechanism
smoothly ticks the planetary orbs through their
circular dance to the strains of an elegant minuet.
The revolving planets are INTERCUT with tight shots of
swirling, dignified 18th Century FIGURES dancing the
minuet in a mirrored ballroom. Over this appears the
following:

Eighteenth Century Europe

The Age of Reason

Mankind enters a new era of scientific

progress, enlightenment and order.

As the DANCERS and planets spin, the orrery continues
to swing the earth slowly towards CAMERA where ... it
explodes. As the smoke clears we see we are looking
into the mouth of an ornate Turkish cannon.

CUT TO:

A RUBBLE-FILLED STREET where the missile from the
Turkish cannon lands and explodes, blowing up a
passing CITIZEN and sending other CITIZENS running for
cover amidst a shower of burning debris.

CUT TO:
THE TURKISH CANNON as they continue to fire. Exotic
flags flutter above them.

### TITLE

THE ADVENTURES OF BARON MUNCHAUSEN

BEGIN CREDITS

**The following sequence was replaced by scenes 13-15 in the final shooting script:**

INT.      THE SULTAN'S HAREM      DAY

ANGLE ON the SULTAN's harem as the BARON and SULTAN
withdraw from the window. The SULTAN, dramatically,
sets up an hourglass. The BARON produces his own
mini-hourglass from his waistcoat pocket, and sets it
going simultaneously with the SULTAN's. He then
returns it to his pocket. The BARON and SULTAN then
drink a toast.


EXT.      THE SULTAN'S GIANT CHESS BOARD      DAY

ANGLE ON the SULTAN's giant chess board where he and
the BARON, seated under canopies, are playing giant
chess in which the pieces are living beings. The pawns
are FOOT SOLDIERS with spears, the knight — MOUNTED
CAVALRY, the rooks — heavy cannon manned by LIVERIED
GUNNERS in castellated howdahs on the backs of
elephants. This being the beginning of the game, there
is a complete set of "pieces" in place. Lying in front
of the SULTAN is his TIGER.

                    SULTAN
                 (to a servant)
          My rook to take the Baron's queen's
          knight.

The SERVANT shouts the SULTAN's instructions through a
megaphone whereupon the GUNNER on one of the SULTAN's
"rooks" fires his cannon at one of the BARON's mounted
SOLDIERS. As the smoke clears only a large crater is
left. The BARON looks disgusted.

                    SULTAN
                 (to BARON)
          Check.

The Baron looks at the SULTAN and then at the
hourglass which is now half empty.

                                      DISSOLVE TO:


EXT.      THE SULTAN'S GIANT CHESS BOARD      DAY

The giant chess board nearly half an hour later. There
are now only a few of the BARON's pieces left on the
board. He has been playing a non-lethal game as best
he can.

                                      (CONTINUED)

                              BARON
                        (to the servant)
                  Bishop to Queen's rook 6.

The SERVANT shouts the BARON's instructions and a
terrified "pawn" shuffles forward onto the next
square.

                              BARON
              Checkmate.

The SULTAN smiles acknowledgement to the BARON and
then glances down at the now nearly empty hourglass.
The BARON looks around at the SULTAN'S EXECUTIONER, a
fat sweaty man with a large shiny scimitar. The
EXECUTIONER, with the help of an ASSISTANT, begins
measuring the preparing the BARON's neck by drawing a
dotted line around it. The BARON checks his personal
hourglass, and glances at BERTHOLD's weights.

                              BARON
              Er, excuse me ... Back in five
              minutes.

The BARON gets up and walks out of the SULTAN's sight
with cool dignity.

However, once around the corner, he breaks into a
desperate run down an arched corridor towards a
distant opening.


**EXT.     SULTAN'S PALACE     DAY**

The BARON hurtles out of an opening in the wall and
leaps high into the air over the balustrading.

                                              CUT TO:

A WIDE SHOT to reveal the opening to be a couple of
hundred feet above the ground. As the BARON falls he
shouts:

                              BARON
              Bucephalus!


                                          (CONTINUED)

**EXT.     A FOUNTAIN SQUARE IN THE GROUNDS OF THE
          SULTAN'S PALACE      DAY**

BUCEPHALUS, the BARON's white stallion, looks up from
the fountain he is drinking from.

**EXT.     SULTAN'S PALACE      DAY**

The BARON plummets down, down, down.

**EXT.     CONSTANTINOPLE STREET      DAY**

BUCEPHALUS thunders down the street as PASSERS-BY leap
out of the way.

**EXT.     SULTAN'S PALACE      DAY**

The BARON continues to fall ... through a line of
laundry ... acquiring another pair of trousers over
the original pair.

**EXT.     ANOTHER STREET IN CONSTANTINOPLE      DAY**

BUCEPHALUS pounds past.

**EXT.     SULTAN'S PALACE      DAY**

And still, the BARON falls — crashing through more
laundry lines — acquiring more odd bits of clothing.

**EXT.     ANOTHER STREET      DAY**

BUCEPHALUS races along ... is he beginning to look
worried?

**EXT.     SULTAN'S PALACE      DAY**

The BARON is looking ever so slightly worried as he
continues his rushing descent. His P.O.V. shows the
ground getting terribly close.

**EXT.     BASE OF SULTAN'S PALACE     DAY**

The BARON hurtles toward the ground with no hope of
averting disaster when ... past CAMERA gallops
BUCEPHALUS — just in time for the BARON to land
squarely in the saddle — and roar off through an
archway.

**EXT.     ANOTHER STREET     DAY**

The BARON and BUCEPHALUS charge around a corner — up
to CAMERA and then take off over us with a mighty
leap.

**EXT.     RICHLY DECORATED WINDOW**

BUCEPHALUS (with BARON) leaps through window.

**INT.     SULTAN'S HAREM     DAY**

BUCEPHALUS and BARON crash through window and gallop
through harem, across pool, past colonnade and out
window.

**EXT.     A SQUARE IN GROUNDS OF SULTAN'S PALACE     DAY**

The BARON'S SERVANTS look up from their card game as
they hear the crash of window. CUT TO their P.O.V. as
they see BUCEPHALUS and BARON come hurtling out of a
window some 40-50 feet above them. With a shrug as if
this is merely typical behavior on the part of the
BARON, they turn back to their game as the BARON and
BUCEPHALUS thunder down to the ground.

                         BARON
                      (breathless)
              Where the hell's Berthold?!

137

**This sequence was replaced by scenes 45-51 in the final shooting script:**

**EXT.     A HARBOR ON THE MOON     DAY**

The BARON and SALLY sail past a gigantic wall from
where a bridge extends to a gigantic lighthouse. They
round a corner and see a vast baroque floating city
into which they continue along a canal of sand. This
brings them to a giant quay.

**EXT.     QUAYSIDE     MOON     DAY**

The BARON and SALLY are mooring the galleon to the
quay, alongside the giant moon-ships. They tie their
thin earth rope around a massive capstan, adding it to
the thick moon ropes already there.

> BARON
> I've always been one of the king's
> favorites ... We'll receive a right
> royal welcome.

Suddenly, the BARON and SALLY and the area immediately
surrounding them are thrown into shadow. They turn
around in search of the cause, and look upwards. Sally
is astonished.

**EXT.     UPPER QUAYSIDE     MOON     DAY**

There, something huge and flapping and emitting a
terrible cacophonous shrieking is diving out of the
sky towards them. It lands in a whirlwind of dust.
Coughing and gagging SALLY and the BARON peer through
the clearing dust. Three gigantic bird-like heads,
their beaks snapping and shrieking, lunge towards
them. SALLY grabs the BARON for protection. As the
dust continues to clear we can see that the heads all
attach to the same body. However, they seem unhappy
with the situation — spending as much time attacking
each other as they do snapping at SALLY and the BARON.
Sitting on the three-headed GRIFFIN's back, trying to
rein in the shrieking heads, is a giant SOLDIER, armed
with an asparagus spear and a mushroom shield.

**EXT.     QUAYSIDE     MOON     DAY**

ANGLE ON the BARON and SALLY where they stand,
dwarfed, at the taloned feet of the huge GRIFFIN.

(CONTINUED)

>           BARON
>         (shouting up)
>     Good morning! I am Baron Munchausen.
>     You may have heard of me ... I'm a
>     very close friend of your king, and
>     I'd be most grateful if you would
>     inform him of my arrival.
>         (to SALLY)
>     Note the asparagus spear. Very
>     effective if used skillfully.

**EXT.     QUAYSIDE     MOON     DAY**

A wide shot of the scene on the quay as the SOLDIER
lifts his asparagus spear and hurls it into the
galleon which instantly sinks beneath the sand.

**INT.     IMPRESSIVE HALL     MOON     DAY**

A magnificent Baroque Hall. Not a soul is in sight.
Off CAMERA a door opens. Footsteps. A FOOTMAN carrying
a tray with a glass cover walks into SHOT ... upside
down on the ceiling! As he crosses the hall the CAMERA
revolves — turning the room upside down but, the
FOOTMAN the right way up. A tighter SHOT reveals a
tiny BARON and SALLY sitting on the giant tray. SALLY
looks apprehensive.

>           BARON
>     They look at things differently here.

The 50-foot-high FOOTMAN continues on through a
massive door.

**INT.     THE ROYAL BANQUETING HALL     MOON     DAY**

As they pass through the door, the floor seems to drop
away. They find themselves on the brink of an enormous
bowl-shaped space.

A banquet is in full swing in the giant KING's
banqueting hall. Giant MUSIC is being played. Giant
GUESTS sit around tables which are groaning with
masses of giant food. Giant FOOTMEN and MAIDS come and
go, pouring wine and waiting on table. Everybody is
having a wonderful time, and everybody and everything
is labelled with a description of what he, she, or it

(CONTINUED)

is. On seeing the BARON and SALLY arrive, the KING,
who is seated at the top of the center table, detaches
his head form his body and sends it to greet them.

> KING'S HEAD
> (zooming through the
> hall)
> Baron! ... Baron Munchausen!

The FOOTMAN lifts the lid from the tray.

> BARON
> (bowing)
> Your Majesty.

> KING'S HEAD
> How marvelous to see you again!

> BARON
> (remembering)
> You remembered.

> KING'S HEAD
> Nobody forgets the Baron ...

The BARON introduces SALLY to the KING'S HEAD.

> BARON
> Sally ... The King ... Well, his head
> at any rate.

> SALLY
> (curtseying)
> How-do-you-do.

> KING'S HEAD
> Charmed I'm sure.
> (to the footman's
> head)
> Label our new guests immediately.

The FOOTMAN's head nods, disconnects from his body and
hovers off. SALLY looks puzzled.

> BARON
> They forget everything whenever
> there's an eclipse.

(CONTINUED)

                              KING'S HEAD
                         (straining to
                         remember)
                    You know, there's something in
                    particular about you, Baron, which I
                    feel I ought to remember ... What on
                    moon is it?
                         (shakes his head)
                    Never mind. Come and join us. You've
                    arrived in time for the great monthly
                    feast of the forgetting.

                                                      CUT TO:

A STAGE at the other end of the banqueting hall on
which a group of giant MUSICIANS accompany four
SINGERS who do a song and dance routine with a great
deal of choreography for detachable heads.

                         THE FOUR HEADS
                         (singing)
                    It's nice to remember the nice things,
                    It's nice to remember what's nice,
                    It's nice to remember the nice things,
                    But it's even nicer to forget.

                    Too much remembering, too much
                       remembering brings you down,
                    To much remembering, too much
                       remembering makes you frown.

                    It's nice to remember ...
                         (etc.)

                                                      CUT TO:

THE BARON AND SALLY who are seated at the top table at
the opposite end to the KING. They are sitting on
chairs, stacked with books, which brings them up to
the level of the other (giant) GUESTS. The BARON now
has a label attached to him reading "Munchausen,
Baron," and SALLY has a label tied to her reading
"Salt, Sally." SALLY is eating like mad, tearing at
items of giant food.

                              SALLY
                         (worried)
                    But what if we forget? ...

                                                (CONTINUED)
                              141

CONTINUED:

                         BARON
          We won't forget. We'll leave before
          the eclipse.

                         SALLY
                    (not satisfied)
          Why didn't you say anything about this
          forgetting business before?

                         BARON
          I forgot.

                         SALLY
                    (putting foot down)
          We can't stay here! There isn't time!

                         BARON
                    (soothingly)
          The city's perfectly all right. The
          present assault is over. Everyone
          there is quite safe.

                         SALLY
          How do you know?

                         BARON
          I just know.

                                              CUT TO:

A VERY QUICK SCENE of ferocious hand-to-hand fighting
along the city walls as waves of TURKS swarm up
ladders and over the battlements and attack the
DEFENDERS.

                                              CUT TO:

SALLY who is looking at the BARON, skeptically.

                                              CUT TO:

THE FOUR HEADS on stage.

                         THE FOUR HEADS
                    (singing)
          Too much remembering, too much
             remembering spoils your day.
          Too much remembering, too much
             remembering turns you grey.
                    (MORE)

                                          (CONTINUED)
                         142

> THE FOUR HEADS (CONT.)
> It's nice to remember ...
> (etc.)

CUT TO:

A WIDE SHOT of the top table where the KING and his
GUESTS are all laughing and knocking back huge goblets
of wine filled from an enormous punch bowl in the
center of the table.

ANGLE ON the BARON and SALLY who are trying to cope
with giant bowls of mushroom soup which have labels
floating in them saying "soup." SALLY has relaxed and
is now enjoying herself.

> ARIADNE (V.O.)
> (sexily)
> Baron!

The BARON and SALLY look up form their soup.

> BARON
> Ariadne!

ANGLE ON ARIADNE as she sits down in the vacant place next
to the BARON. She is very beautiful, extremely sexy, is
wearing a coronet and a low cut dress and is gigantic.

> ARIADNE
> How thrilling.

> BARON
> (bowing)
> Your majesty. The pleasure is all
> mine.

SALLY, jealous and impatient, clears her throat
noisily. The BARON introduces her to ARIADNE.

> BARON
> Sally ... Sally Salt ... Queen
> Ariadne.

At this point the BARON, SALLY and ARIADNE are
distracted by a loud burst of laughter and cheers from
further up the table.

ANGLE ON the KING and his GUESTS who we see are all
laughing at the PRIME MINISTER who is clearly very drunk.

(CONTINUED)

                    PRIME MINISTER
                        (drunk)
          An astronomer chappie called Smith
          Thought the man in the moon was a
          myth.
          But while seeking the truth
          He fell off the roof
          Broke his neck and was buried
          forthwith.
                        (with apologies to
                        M. Palin)

The PRIME MINISTER's head falls off his shoulders and
into the punch bowl. The KING and his GUESTS fall
about at the sight of the drunken PRIME MINISTER's
head scooting around the punch bowl, choking and
spitting out fountains of wine. A couple of SERVANTS
fish out the half-drowned head and set it on the
table.

ANGLE ON the KING as he raises his glass in salute to
the BARON.

ANGLE ON the BARON as he attempts to return the KING's
salute with his giant goblet of wine. He has to climb
onto the table in order to pick up the glass. The
BARON manages, with difficulty, to return the KING's
salute, but soaks himself with wine in the process.

ANGLE ON the KING and his GUESTS who are laughing at
the BARON and enjoying the show he's providing with
the giant goblet.

ANGLE ON the soaked BARON as he bows to the king.
SALLY laughs.

ANGLE ON ARIADNE as she dips a finger in the puddle of
spilt wine and slowly licks it off her finger. She
smiles seductively at the BARON. She then picks a few
grapes from one of the platters and, while maintaining
eye contact with the BARON, eats them lasciviously.
She then flicks a grape to the BARON.

ANGLE ON the BARON as he catches the grapes from
ARIADNE. He tries to bite into it but can't break the
skin with his teeth. The BARON then climbs onto the
table again and attempts to cut open the grape with
his giant knife. This doesn't work either. He looks
towards ARIADNE and smiles.

                                            (CONTINUED)

ANGLE ON ARIADNE as she continues to eat grapes and look meaningfully at the BARON.

ANGLE ON the BARON as he gives up trying to break into his grape with the unwieldy giant knife, and begins stamping on it. This rapidly leads him to showing off his soccer skills and expertly juggling the grape with his feet, and keeping it in the air.

ANGLE ON ARIADNE who is delighted with the BARON's impressive performance.

ANGLE ON SALLY who looks disgusted. She throws down her giant fork. This causes the BARON to momentarily lose his concentration, and accidentally kick the grape towards ARIADNE.

ANGLE ON ARIADNE as the grape shoots towards her and disappears into her cleavage.

ANGLE ON the BARON and SALLY. SALLY buries her face in her hands with shame, and the BARON rushes towards ARIADNE to retrieve the grape.

ANGLE ON ARIADNE as the BARON dives into her cleavage in pursuit of the grape. After a struggle, which ARIADNE enjoys quite a lot, the triumphant BARON emerges from between her breasts with the grape between his teeth. The BARON is very pleased with himself, but ARIADNE suddenly sees something beyond him and is frightened.

THE CAMERA pulls back to reveal the KING'S HEAD hovering behind the BARON. The KING is seething with jealousy and anger. The BARON fails to notice him for a moment until he sees SALLY trying to signal a warning, and becomes aware of ARIADNE's expression and the fact that the banqueting hall has become silent. At last the BARON turns to the KING.

> KING
> Now I remember! ... You tried to steal
> my queen the last time you were here!

### INT.     CAGE IN CELL     MOON     DAY

The BARON and SALLY are in a large cage (about the size of a giant's head), suspended, high up, from a hook in a wall. There are a couple of empty cages next to theirs.

(CONTINUED)

                              SALLY
                            (furious)
                    How stupid!

                              BARON
                    If you hadn't distracted me, I
                    wouldn't have kicked that grape ...

                              SALLY
                    You shouldn't have flirted with her in
                    the first place!

                              BARON
                    I was merely being polite.

                              SALLY
                    We've got to escape before the
                    eclipse! ... If we do forget
                    everything ...

                              PRIME MINISTER (V.O.)
                    Don't worry about a thing ...

The BARON and SALLY look across the cell to another wall.

                                                    CUT TO:

A WIDE SHOT of the cell. We see that there are dozens
of cages hung around the walls and that many of them
contain the heads of PRISONERS. The PRISONERS' bodies
are chained to the walls and floor beneath the cages.
The PRIME MINISTER's head is in one of the cages.

                              PRIME MINISTER
                    Once you've forgotten ... you've
                    forgotten. It's very soothing.

                              SALLY
                    How can we get out of here?

                              PRIME MINISTER
                    No need. We'll be in the eclipse in a
                    moment.
He nods towards a window through which can be seen the
approaching shadow of the eclipse sweeping across the
buildings of the palace.

                              PRIME MINISTER
                    After that ... no responsibilities, no
                            (MORE)

                                                    (CONTINUED)

                         PRIME MINISTER (CONT.)
           worries, no guilt, no hangover ... a
           clean slate. You'll be very happy.

                         SALLY
    We don't want to forget!

                         PRIME MINISTER
    If you take my advice ...

At this point the shadow of the eclipse falls through
the window and onto the PRIME MINISTER.

                         PRIME MINISTER
    Hup! ...
             (mumbling
             blissfully)
    Who? ... Where? ... I? ... You? ...
    Why? ... Who I? ... Where I? ... Where
    who? ... Who I? ... What why? ... Why
    what? ...
             (etc.)

ANGLE ON the BARON and SALLY.

                         SALLY
    Come on! If we climb along here, we
    can jump down onto one of those
    bodies.

The BARON is irritated by SALLY taking over and
bossing him about. SALLY slips through the bars of the
cage, and steps across the void into the next cage.
The BARON, who has some difficulty squeezing between
the bars, follows her. This new cage is littered with
giant straw, and the BARON steps into a pile of it as
he enters.

                         VOICE
             (from under the
             straw)
    Ow!

The BARON springs away and draws his saber.

                         BARON
    Come out! ... Come out of there,
    whoever you are!

Since nothing happens, the BARON prods the straw with

                                   (CONTINUED)

his saber.

                    VOICE
          Ow! Stop that!

An OLD MAN with a long white beard and hair stands up
from under the straw.

                    OLD MAN
                (indignant)
          What'd you do that for?!!!

                    BARON
          I'm sorry, I thought you might be
          unfriendly.

                    OLD MAN
          Of course I'm unfriendly! You'd be
          unfriendly if I prodded you!

                    SALLY
          Who are you?

                    OLD MAN
                (thinks)
          Hang on! I used to have a label here
          somewhere ...

The OLD MAN begins to rummage in the straw in search
of his label.

                    OLD MAN
                (finding label)
          Here we are.
                (showing label to
                SALLY)
          What's it say?

                    SALLY
                (reading)
          "Label."

                    SALLY
                (upset, to the
                BARON)
          We'll be like him if we don't escape!

                    BARON
          Why are you in here?

(CONTINUED)

                    148

                    OLD MAN
          I'm a very wicked criminal.

                    SALLY
          What have you done?

                    OLD MAN
          I can't remember.

                    SALLY
          Then how do you know you're very
          wicked?

                    OLD MAN
          Well, for one thing ... I'm in here.
          And for another ... I've got these
          shackles on.

The OLD MAN steps out of the straw dragging shackles
with him. These are in fact BERTHOLD's weights.

                    BARON
                 (excited)
          Berthold!!!

                    BERTHOLD
                 (for it is he)
          Eh?

                    BARON
                 (to SALLY)
          It's Berthold!!!

The BARON leaps forward and embraces BERTHOLD.
(BERTHOLD is played, once again, by DESMOND from
Salt's theater company, but this time not in heavy
theatrical make-up. In other words he is more "real"
as BERTHOLD than he was in the Sultan's Tale. He is
also much older.)

                    BARON
          Berthold! It's me! ... The Baron! I
          knew I'd find you on the moon! We've
          come to take you back to earth!

BERTHOLD tries to fight off the BARON's embraces.

                    BERTHOLD
          Get off! ... Get off me! ...

                                        (CONTINUED)
                    149

> BARON
>
> You're Berthold, Berthold my old
> servant. Those leg irons are to slow
> you down ... Stop you tearing off all
> over the place ...

> BERTHOLD
>
> You must be joking.

> BARON
>
> You always wore them ... Remember?

> BERTHOLD
>
> You're crackers.

> BARON
>
> I'm Baron Munchausen.

> BERTHOLD
>
> That sounds nasty. Is it contagious?

> SALLY
>
> We're wasting time! The shadow's
> getting closer!

At this point we hear the sound of a key turning in
the cell door lock.

> BERTHOLD
>
> The jailer! Get down! He's a brute!

BERTHOLD dives under giant straw. The BARON and SALLY
crouch down on the floor of the cage.

CUT TO:

THE BARON AND SALLY's P.O.V. of the cell door as it
creaks slowly open. After a moment, ARIADNE's detached
head hovers in.

> BARON
> (delighted)
>
> Ariadne?

> ARIADNE
> (sotto voce)
>
> Shhh! We mustn't alert the guards!

ARIADNE'S head zooms up the cage.

(CONTINUED)

> ARIADNE
> Darling Baron ... You're much too
> handsome to languish in jail ...

> BARON
> Where's the king?

> ARIADNE
> He's in bed with my body
> > (orgasmic)
> Ooooh ... Stop it! ... But if he
> discovers that my head's with you ...
> Ahhh ... Quickly, climb into my hair!
> Ooooaaahh! Ooooaaaeee!

ARIADNE positions her head against the bars of the cage.

> SALLY
> > (aside to BARON)
> Why is she making those funny noises?

> BARON
> > (embarrassed)
> Her body's with the King and ... he's
> tickling her feet.
> > (turning quickly to
> > BERTHOLD)
> Berthold!

The BARON drags BERTHOLD out of the pile of giant straw.

> BARON
> Come on!

> BERTHOLD
> > (struggling)
> Let go of me! ...

> BARON
> You're coming with us.

> BERTHOLD
> No chance!

> BARON
> Why not?

> BERTHOLD
> > (thinks)
> Can't remember.

(CONTINUED)

CONTINUED:

                           BARON
              You're not frightened are you?

                         BERTHOLD
           That's it!

                           BARON
                         (to SALLY)
           Help me.

The BARON and SALLY bundle the struggling BERTHOLD
through the bars of the cage and onto ARIADNE's head,
where they all cling on to her hair.

                                                 CUT TO:

A WIDE SHOT of the cell as ARIADNE's head zips down
from the cage and out through the door. As this
happens, those giant PRISONERS in the cell who haven't
yet been eclipsed become aware of the fact that an
escape is taking place and begin shouting.

                       GIANT PRISONERS
           Hey, what about us? Take us with you!
           Don't go without us! They're escaping!
                          (etc.)

**INT.       PASSAGE OUTSIDE CELL      MOON      DAY**

Outside the giant cell door as ARIADNE's head, with
the BARON and CO. in her hair, zips out into the
passage. A second later, a giant JAILER's head comes
out of the guard room at the far end of the passage.

                       JAILER'S HEAD
              What's going on down there!

The JAILER's head turns and whistles back into the
guard room.

                       JAILER'S HEAD
                         (whistles)

The JAILER's head then rockets down the passage,
towards the cell. A moment later, his body races out
of the guard room in hot pursuit of the head. The body
catches up with the head and joins it just in time for
them to run into the cell as one.

                            152

**INT.     CELLS     MOON     DAY**

The JAILER halts inside the door.

> JAILER
> Who opened this door?

Through the door behind him we see ARIADNE's head dart
across the opening. The door slams shut.

**INT.     PASSAGE OUTSIDE CELL     MOON     DAY**

ARIADNE'S head turns the key with her teeth. This
action nearly dislodges the BARON and CO. From inside
the cell the JAILER hammers on the door and shouts, as
ARIADNE's head with the BARON and CO. on board zooms
off down the passage.

**INT.     STONE PASSAGES IN PALACE     MOON     DAY**

ANGLE ON ARIADNE's head with the BARON and CO. on it
as she zooms along a series of stone passages.

> ARIADNE
> I'll take you to the Cheddar Gate ...
> You can get out there ... after that
> you're on your ownnnnnnnnoooaaaaaaaa!

ARIADNE's head reaches a junction in the passages and
turns a corner. Here she finds herself in a passage
along which the eclipse shadow is approaching. A
couple of headless BODIES, limbs akimbo, rush wildly
past. The area already in shadow is full of inert
BODIES and even more inert HEADS.

> HEADS
> (blissfully)
> I? ... What? ... Where? ... Where I?
> ... Am I? ... Am what? ... Who is? ...
> What where? ...

> ARIADNE
> The eclipse! ... Ooooooooh? ... We'll
> have to go another way!

ARIADNE's head turns and runs straight into the chest
of a giant GUARD. The GUARD tries to grab hold of her
but she ducks and weaves her way past him. The GUARD

(CONTINUED)

CONTINUED:

plus two other GUARDS chase after her.

INT.     **STONE PASSAGES IN PALACE     MOON**

ANGLE ON the three GUARDS as they charge around a
corner. The LEADER trips over something and falls to
the ground.

>                    IAN
>              (falling)
>          Ow! Shit!

The two other GUARDS stop to help him up, and we see
that he has tripped over a giant marble head.

>                    ROBERT
>          You all right?

>                    IAN
>              (angry)
>          No!

>                    ARIADNE (V.O.)
>          Ooooooaaa!

>                    IAN
>          What's that?

We now see that the GUARDS are standing in a corridor
full of pieces of giant marble statues of moon-people;
heads, hands, feet, etc. Behind them is a stack of
upside down statues, some of whose heads are close to
and on a level with the GUARDS' heads. As the GUARDS
pause to listen, we PAN IN to discover that the head
of one of these statues is missing and that its place
has been taken by ARIADNE's head which is hovering
upside down in the hope of being mistaken for part of
the statue. The BARON and CO. are hiding behind her.

>                    ARIADNE
>          Mnnnnoaahh!

The BARON, SALLY and BERTHOLD exchange fearful looks.

>                    IAN
>          There it is again.

The BARON hurriedly removes his jacket, and, risking
being seen, stuffs if as quickly as possible into

(CONTINUED)

CONTINUED:

ARIADNE's mouth before returning to cover.

The GUARDS listen for a moment.

                    ROBERT
          I can't hear anything.

                    IAN
     Sshh!

ARIADNE is straining to explode, but the BARON's coat
is just about keeping her quiet. The BARON, SALLY and
BERTHOLD watch her anxiously.

                    FRANK
                 (fed up)
          They've gone. They're miles away by
          now. What's the point of chasing them
          anyway?

                    ROBERT
          Right ... We're gonna forget
          everything in five minutes.

                    IAN
          That's why I want to catch 'em,
          stupid! Do something *really* nasty
          what's worth forgetting.
                 (moving off)
          Come on!

The GUARDS run off. The BARON and CO. emerge from
behind ARIADNE just in time for her to explode and
blow the BARON's coat out of her mouth at the BARON.


**EXT.     CLOISTERS ON MOON     DAY**

ARIADNE's head, the BARON, SALLY and BERTHOLD enter a
giant unfinished cloister. A giant headless BODY is
gambolling on the grass in the middle of the
quadrangle, leaping about, rolling over, and doing
silly things.

                    ARIADNE
          Ooooaaaaahh ... ! I must leave you.
                 (nodding towards the
                 other side of the quad)
          The Cheddar Gate's over there.
                 (MORE)

**155**

                    ARIADNE (CONT.)
                 (suddenly passionate)
        Oh Baron ... Darling ... take me with
        you.

                    BARON
                 (taken aback)
        My dear ... Back to earth?

                    ARIADNE
        Yes.

                    BARON
        Er ... Without your body?

                    ARIADNE
                 (hurt)
        I thought you loved me for myself?

                    BARON
        Oh I did, I do, of course I do.

                    SALLY
                 (sick of this)
        We've got to go!

                    ARIADNE
        No, you're right, it's impossible ...
        It was just a mad thought ... Here.
        Take a lock of my hair.

The BARON takes out his saber and cuts a 6-foot lock
of ARIADNE's hair which he ties around his neck like a
long scarf.

                    BERTHOLD
        Just a lock cocky! Not the whole
        carpet!

                    BARON
        I shall treasure it, always.

                    ARIADNE
        Ooooooooooh ... ! Aaaaaaaaaaaaah ...!
        The king's ... Haaaaaaaaaaaaaaa ... !
        I must go back ... OOOOOOOOOOOH ...!
        Au revoir dear Baron ... AAAAAAH ... !
        I hope we'll meet again ...
        OO, OO, OO, OO, AAH! Good luck!
        AAAAAAAAAAAAAAAH!

                                        (CONTINUED)

CONTINUED:

The BARON plucks a red paper rose from inside his
jacket and puts it between ARIADNE's teeth.

ARIADNE's head shoots off around the quadrangle, out
of sight.

> ARIADNE
> I'm coming Roger ... I'm coming ...
> OOOOOOOOOOAAAAAAAAAOOOOOOOOOOO ... !

**EXT.      CHEDDAR GATE      MOON      DAY**

The BARON, SALLY and BERTHOLD arrive at an impressive
portal one side of the cloistered quadrangle. This
leads out to the open moon, a vast desert space
littered with unfinished buildings. Behind the BARON
and CO., in the middle of the quadrangle, the giant
headless BODY continues to frolic. A giant female
HEAD, set in the top of the arch of the portal, sees
the BARON and CO.

> PORTAL HEAD
> Three escaped prisoners at the Cheddar
> Gate! ... Three escaped prisoners ...
> (etc.)

The BARON and CO. look around, panic stricken. Bells
begin to ring.

> BARON
> This way! And don't run into the
> shade!

The BARON and CO. look around, panic stricken. Bells
begin to ring.

**INT.      THE KING'S BEDROOM      MOON      DAY**

ANGLE ON the KING, who is tickling the QUEEN's feet.
The QUEEN's body is writhing under the bedclothes. The
voice of the PORTAL HEAD blasts through the window.

> PORTAL HEAD
> ... The Cheddar Gate ... Three escaped
> prisoners at the Cheddar Gate.

The KING lifts the bedclothes from the top of the
QUEEN's body to discover that her head is missing.

(CONTINUED)

157

CONTINUED:

                         KING'S HEAD
                         (furious)
             I wondered why you were so quiet! ...
             Your damned head's with the Baron,
             isn't it?!!! ... I'll kill him!!! ...
                         (shouting out of the
                         bedroom door)
             Saddle my griffin!!!


**EXT.    MOONSCAPE ON VERGE OF ECLIPSE**

ANGLE ON the BARON and CO. as they struggle across the
moon, away from the palace, past abandoned, half-
finished buildings and structures. We hear the blast
of a distant hunting horn. The BARON and CO. look back
towards the direction of the palace.

                                             CUT TO:

THE BARON AND CO.'S P.O.V. where we see, hovering over
the palace, a mounted THREE-HEADED GRIFFIN.

                                             CUT TO:

A CLOSE-UP of the GRIFFIN which we discover is being
ridden by the KING, armed with a mushroom shield and
asparagus spear.

                         KING
                         (steadying the
                         griffin)
             Hungry are we, Silver? Go get 'em!

The KING spurs the GRIFFIN, which roars, rears back
and then zooms away with much snarling of flared
nostrils and beating of wings.

# CREDITS

COLUMBIA PICTURES

Presents

A PROMINENT FEATURES/LAURA FILM PRODUCTION
A TERRY GILLIAM FILM

## "THE ADVENTURES OF BARON MUNCHAUSEN"

JOHN NEVILLE
ERIC IDLE
SARAH POLLEY
OLIVER REED
UMA THURMAN
JONATHAN PRYCE
Special Appearance by VALENTINA CORTESE

Original Score by MICHAEL KAMEN
Photography by GIUSEPPE ROTUNNO (AIC) (ASC)
Edited by PETER HOLLYWOOD
Production Designer DANTE FERRETTI
Special Effects by RICHARD CONWAY
Costumes by GABRIELLA PESCUCCI
Screenplay by CHARLES McKEOWN & TERRY GILLIAM
Executive Producer JAKE EBERTS
Co-Producer RAY COOPER
Supervising Producer STRATTON LEOPOLD
Line Producer DAVID TOMBLIN
Produced by THOMAS SCHUHLY
Directed by TERRY GILLIAM
Original Soundtrack Album Available on
Warner Bros. Records, Tapes and Compact Discs

Credits as of 2/9/89

# THE CAST

Baron Munchausen ..................................................... JOHN NEVILLE
Desmond/Berthold ......................................................... ERIC IDLE
Sally Salt ..................................................................... SARAH POLLEY
Vulcan ............................................................................ OLIVER REED
Rupert/Adolphus .............................................. CHARLES McKEOWN
Bill/Albrecht ........................................................ WINSTON DENNIS
Jeremy/Gustavus ................................................................ JACK PURVIS
Queen Ariadne/Violet ...................................... VALENTINA CORTESE
Horatio Jackson ........................................................ JONATHAN PRYCE
Henry Salt .................................................................... BILL PATERSON
The Sultan ...................................................................... PETER JEFFREY
Venus/Rose .................................................................. UMA THURMAN
Daisy ........................................................................ ALISON STEADMAN
Functionary ...................................................................... RAY COOPER
Commander ............................................................. DON HENDERSON
Heroic Officer ............................................................................. STING
Colonel ..................................................... ANDREW MACLACHLAN
Dr. Death ...................................................................... JOSE LIFANTE
Executioner ............................................ MOHAMED BADRESALEM
King of the Moon ..................................................... RAY D. TUTTO
Executioner's Assistant ........................................... KIRAN SHAH
Treasurer .................................................................. FRANCO ADDUCCI
First General ............................................................... ETTORE MARTINI
Second General ....................................................... ANTONIO PISTILLO
Gunners ............................................................... MICHAEL POLLEY
TONY SMART

# THE CREDITS

Directed by .................................................................. TERRY GILLIAM

Produced by ............................................................ THOMAS SCHUHLY

Line Producer .............................................................. DAVID TOMBLIN

Supervising Producer ........................................ STRATTON LEOPOLD

Executive Producer ............................................................ JAKE EBERTS

Co-Producer ........................................................................ RAY COOPER

Screenplay by ................... CHARLES McKEOWN & TERRY GILLIAM

Music by .................................................................... MICHAEL KAMEN

Director of Photography ................. GIUSEPPE ROTUNNO, AIC, ASC

Production Designer ..................................................... DANTE FERRETTI

Editor ................................................................... PETER HOLLYWOOD

Costume Designer ........................................... GABRIELLA PESCUCCI

Make-up & Hair Designed by ................................... MAGGIE WESTON

Make-up ................................................................. FABRIZIO SFORZA

Special Effects .......................................................... RICHARD CONWAY

Optical Effects by .............. PEERLESS CAMERA CO. LTD. LONDON

Casting ............................................................................. IRENE LAMB
                                         MARGERY SIMKIN
                                   FRANCESCO CINIERI

Supervising Art Director ........................................... MASSIMO RAZZI

Art Director .............................................................. TERESA BARBASSO

Set Decorator ............................................. FRANCESCA LO SCHIAVO

Production Controller .................................................. ARTHUR TARRY

Production Executive ................................................. JOYCE HERLIHY

Executive in Charge of Production .... ROBERT GORDON EDWARDS
                               CINEMA PRODUCTION CONSULTANTS

(MORE)

# CREDITS (CONT.)

Production Supervisor ......................................................... MARIO PISANI

Production Manager (Spain) .............................FRANCISCO MOLERO

Production Manager (Italy) ...................................................... PINO BUTI

Unit Manager (Italy) ...................................... VITTORIO FORNASIERO

Unit Manager (Spain) ...................................FERNANDO MARQUERIE

First Assistant Directors...................................................... JOHN COZZO
LEE CLEARY

Assistant Director (Italy).................................................. LUCA LACHIN

Assistant Director (Spain) .....................................JOSE LUIS ESCOLAR

Script Supervisor...................................................................NIKKI CLAPP

Production Coordinators ................................... NANCY RUBIN LEVIN
SUSANA PRIETO
GAIL SAMUELSON

Assistant to Producer ......................................... DANIELA EDELBURG

Production Secretary .........................................................LISA DASTEEL

Assistant to Terry Gilliam.........................................NYLA VAN INGEN

Dialogue Coach ...................................................................... JAN GREEN

Camera Operator.............................................................FRANCO BRUNI

First Assistant Camera ............................... GIANMARIA MAJORANA

Special Assistants Camera ...........................................DANIELE CIMINI
GIOVANNI PIPERNO

Key Grip ....................................................................... ALDO COLANZI

Video Operator....................................................................... IAN KELLY

Production Sound Mixer...................................................FRANK JAHN

Boom Operators .........................................................RAYMOND MEYER
GUNTHER RUCKDESCHEL

(MORE)

# CREDITS (CONT.)

Art Directors ...................................................... GIORGIO GIOVANNINI
NAZZARENO PIANA

Supervising Painter....................................................SANTE BARELLI

Assistant Set Decorators................................... GIOVANNI PASSANISI
ATOS MASTROGIROLAMO

Property Master.............................................. GIANNI FIUME
CHARLES TORBETT

Property Buyer ........................................... BRUNO TEMPERA

Make-up & Hair ................................................. PAM MEAGER

Hairdresser Supervisor (Italy)..................................... IOLE CECCHINI

Hairdressers...........................................................GIANCARLO MARIN
CARLA INDONI
ELISABETTA DE LEONARDIS

Make-up Artists............................................... ANTONIO MALTEMPO
ENRICO IACOPONI
ALFREDO TIBERI
GINO TAMAGNINI
CHRISTINA DE ROSSI

Assistants to Costume Designer ..............................CARLO POGGIOLI
ALBERTO SPIAZZI
ALFONSA LETTIERI

Wardrobe Master ...................................................... GREGORIO SIMILI

Wardrobe Mistress................................................ IRENE SANTARELLI

Wardrobe Assistant .................................................... CELESTE FRANZI

Accountant (Italy) ...................................................................ENZO SISTI

Accountant (Spain) ...........................................SANTIAGO DE BENITO

Assistant Accountants............................................ PAULINE GRANBY
ALBERTO DE STEFANI
CARLA ZACCHIA
LUIDI CAMACHO

(MORE)

## CREDITS (CONT.)

| | |
|---|---|
| Assistant Accountants (Cont.)............................ | LEANDRO MUSLERA |
| | MARIA FIORITO |
| Associate Editor............................................................ | CHRIS BLUNDEN |
| Special Effects Editor ........................................................ | BRIAN MANN |
| Supervising Sound Editor............................................. | PETER PENNELL |
| Sound Editors ................................................................. | COLIN MILLER |
| | PETER HORROCKS |
| | BOB RISK |
| | RUSTY COPPLEMAN |
| Assistant Editors ......................................................... | STEVE MAGUIRE |
| | BEN PALMER |
| | MARTYN ROBINSON |
| | NATALIE BAKER |
| | STEFNA SMAL |
| | BILL BARRINGER |
| | CHRISTINE NEWELL |
| | MICK MONKS |
| Chief Dubbing Mixer.................................. | GRAHAM V. HARTSTONE |
| Dubbing Mixers............................................. | NICOLAS LE MESSURIER |
| | MICHAEL A. CARTER |
| Special Effects Supervisor (Italy) .................... | ADRIANO PISCHIUTTA |
| Special Effects Supervisor (Spain) ............................ | ANTONIO PARRA |
| Italian Special Effects Technicians.................... | FAUSTO BALDINELLI |
| | LUIGI BATTESTELLI |
| | MICHELE BOREA |
| | BENIAMINO CAROZZA |
| | MARCELLO COCCIA |
| | MARINO ERCA |
| | GIANNI INDOVINO |
| | GIANCARLO MANCINI |
| | MASSIMO NESPOLI |
| | DUILIO OLMI |
| | CLAUDIO SAVASSI |
| | SIMON WEISSE |

(MORE)

# CREDITS (CONT.)

English Special Effects Technicians ......................... NORMAN BAILLIE
CHRISTOPHER COBOULD
PETER DAVEY
JAMIE COURTIER
MARTIN GANT
STEVE HAMILTON
BOB HOLLOW
BRIAN LINCE
DAVE McCALL
TIM WILLIS

Matte Photography Consultants ........................... DENNIS BARTLETT
STANLEY W. SAYER, BSC

Special Effects Plasterer (Animatronics) ............. ALLAN CROUCHER

Special Effects Modellers ................................... VALERIE CHARLTON
CHRISTINE OVERS

Special Effects Wiremen............................................ BOB WIESINGER
KEVIN MATHEWS
BILLY HOWE

Puppeteers................................................................ DAVID BARCLAY
JEFF FELIX

Stunt Coordinator & Horsemaster ................................. TONY SMART

Stunt Coordinator (Italy)......................................... RICCARDO MIONI

Stuntmen ................................................................ BILLY HORRIGAN
LESLIE MARYON
RICCARDO CRUZ MORAL
DINNY POWELL
ANGELO RAGUSA
KIRAN SHAH
JESUS RIARAN TORRES

Choreographers............................................................ PINO PENESSE
GIORGIO ROSSI

Assistant ............................................................ RAFFAELA GIORDANI

(MORE)

Unit Publicists................................................................EUGENE RIZZO
KLAUS SCHUHLY
GRADY CLARKSON

Still Photographers ................................................FRANCO BELLOMO
SERGIO STRIZZI

Production Assistants (Italy) .................................. RICCARDO SPADA
CLAUDIO CORBUCCI

Production Assistants (Spain) ................................MANOLO GARCIA
GONZALO JIMENEZ

Production Secretary (Spain)........................ YOLANDA MARQUERIE

P.A. to Terry Gilliam (U.K.)..................................MARGARITA DOYLE

P.A. to Terry Gilliam (Italy)..........................SALVATORE MURREDU

Assistant to Stratton Leopold ....................................... JANICE MUNRO

Production Runner (Italy)..........................MASSIMILIANO MAZZINI

Production Runner (Spain)...................................TINO TORRESCUSA

Transportation Manager (Italy) ...................................REMO UBERTINI

Transportation Manager (Spain)......................FRANCISCO ARDURA

Supervising Gaffer ......................................................RENATO SARDINI

Electricians ........................................................... GIUSEPPE BERTUCCI
MASSIMO BERTUCCI
MARIO BRAMUCCI
GIUSEPPE FABRIZI
CLAUDIO FROLLANO
GIANNI GENTILI
IGNAZIO MACCARONE
LUCIANO MAROCCHI
GIORGIO PASQUALINI
FRANCESCO QUATTRONE

Construction Manager (Italy)....................................LUIGI SERGIANNI

Construction Manager (Spain)........................................ RAMON MOYA

(MORE)

# CREDITS (CONT.)

Sculpting Supervisor ............................................ FILOMENO CRISARA

Sculpters ....................................................................GIANNI GIANESE
SALVATORE PLACENTI

Construction .............................................. DOMENICO CAPONECCHI
OSVALDO CARUSO
BRUNO COLANZI
SERGIO CONTI
GIANPAOLO MAIORANA
ROBERTO DIAMANTI
MARIO PEZZOTTI
ANGELO TIBERTI
PIETRO SANTARELLI

Music Played by
The Symphony Orchestra Graunke
With
The Chamber Choir "Pro Musika Seria"
Munich
Conducted by
Michael Kamen

Music Recorded & Mixed by .....................STEPHEN MacLAUGHLIN

Orchestral Engineer ....................................................ERIC TOMLINSON

Music Editor...................................................................... CHRIS BROOKS

Music Preparetion...................................................................VIC FRASER

Orchestrations by ..................................................... MICHAEL KAMEN

Additional Orchestrations by................................. FIACHRA TRENCH
JOHN FIDDY
ALAN ARNOLD
ED SHEARMUR
RICK WENTWORTH

Orchestra Manager ................................................ PAUL TALKINGTON

(MORE)

# CREDITS (CONT.)

Music Recorded at
The Bavaria Music Studios, Munich

Soundtrack Available on
Warner Brothers Records

Music Produced by
Michael Kamen   Ray Cooper

"The Torturer's Apprentice"
Music & Lyrics by
Michael Kamen & Eric Idle
Used by the permission of
K Man Corporation & Kay-Gee-Bee Music Limited

Optical Effects & Titling... PEERLESS CAMERA CO. LTD. LONDON

Optical Effects Supervisor .......................................... KENT HOUSTON

Optical Effects Coordinator ............................................ MARTIN BODY

Optical Cameramen ...................................................... NICK DUNLOP
DOUG FORREST
TIM OLLIVE
ANDY JEFFERY
STEVE CUTMORE
LES BROUGHTON
MIKE FERRITER

Rotoscope Artists ................................................................ JANICE BODY
RASHID KHARES

Matte Camera .................................................................... JOHN GRANT

Title Graphics.................................................................... CHRIS ALLIES

Matte Painters................................................................... DOUG FERRIS
JOY CUFF
BOB CUFF
LEIGH TOOK

Motion Control.................................................................. PETER TYLER
KENNETH GRAY

Computer Animation ................ DIGITAL PICTURES LTD. LONDON

(MORE)

# CREDITS (CONT.)

*Second Unit*

| | |
|---|---|
| Director | MICHELE SOAVI |
| Assistant Director (Italy) | CATHERINE VENTURA |
| 1st Assistant Director (Spain) | JAVIER CHINCILLA |
| 2nd Assistant Director (Spain) | JAVIER BALAGUER |
| 3rd Assistant Director (Spain) | MANOLO ZARZO |
| Script Supervisor | YUYI BERINGOLA |
| Production Manager | GIORGIO RUSSO |
| Location Manager (Spain) | PEPE PANERO |
| Production Assistant (Italy) | PAOLO MEROSI |
| Production Secretary (Spain) | DORIANA BONORA |
| Direction of Photography | GIANNI FIORE COLTELLACCI |
| Camera Assistants | ROBERTO MARSIGLI |
| | UMBERTO LUCIGNANO |
| Video Operator | GIOVANNI PIPERNO |
| Chief Make-up Artist (Spain) | FERNANDO PEREZ |
| Make-up Artists (Spain) | JOSE PEREZ |
| | MANUEL MARTIN GONZALEZ |
| Hair Stylist (Spain) | ALICIA REGUERIO |
| Wardrobe Supervisor (Spain) | MARTIN DIAZ |
| Wardrobe Master (Spain) | GIANNI DODDI |
| Special Effects Technician (Spain) | MANOLO GOMEZ |
| Gaffer | SPARTACO SARDINI |
| Chief Grip | ELIO BOSI |
| Stunts (Spain) | EDUARDO GARCIA |
| | JOSE GARCIA |
| | PAQUITO GOMEZ |

(MORE)

Stunts (Spain) (Cont.) ..................................................... LUIS GUTIERREZ
SALVADOR MARIOS
CAMILO VILA NOVOA

*Model Unit*

Director of Photography ................................................... ROGER PRATT

Camera Assistant ....................................................... SIMON FULFORD

Clapper/Loader ..................................................... GRAHAM MARTYR

Camera Grip ................................................................ PETER BUTLER

Art Directors ........................................................ MICHAEL LAMONT
KEN COURT

Assistant Art Director...................................................... MARK HARRIS

Draftsmen.................................................................. DENNIS BOSHER
NEIL LAMONT

Construction Manager........................................... TONY GRAYSMARK

Construction Supervisor ........................................... PETER WILLIAMS

Art Department Assistant........................................... KEITH HORSLEY

Art Department Runner.............................................. SIMON LAMONT

Models Supervisor ........................................................ MARTIN GANT

Special Effects Engineers........................................... LESLIE WHEELER
FRANK GUINEY

Animatronics Model Designers .............................. STEPHEN ONIONS
JAMIE COURTIER
IAN WHITTAKER

Model Makers.................................................................... JIM MACHIN
BRIAN COLE

Sculptors........................................................................ KEITH SHORT
JOHN BLAKELY

Decor Artist................................................................ ROBERT WALKER


(MORE)

172

## CREDITS (CONT.)

Set Decorator.................................................... GILLIAN NOYES COURT

Gaffer ......................................................................................TED READ

Best Boy ..............................................................................PETER LAMB

Electricians ........................................................... VERNON CONNOLLY
STUART KING
BARRY READ

Unit Driver............................................................. JOHN HOLLYWOOD

Produced in association with
Allied Filmmakers
for Prominent Features
Steve Abbott   Anne James
Ian Miles   Pat West
Ralph Kamp   Liz Lehmans

Production Services in Spain by
IMPALA

SPECTRAL RECORDING
DOLBY ® STEREO
IN SELECTED THEATRES

Costumes
Tirelli Costumes (Rome)

Jewels
Nino Lembo (Rome)

Cameras
Technovision ®

Lighting Services
Franco Petracca & Co.
MR Lighting Ltd.

Transport
Tonino Danieli For Romana Transport
(Rome)

(MORE)

CREDITS (CONT.)

Cine-
Citta

Studios
Technical
Equipment
Colour

Originated on
Eastman Color Film from Kodak

Color by
Rank Film Laboratories

Post-Production
Pinewood Studios

With thanks to the people of
Belchite
for their cooperation

With special thanks to
Don French

"Man of the Match"
David Tomblin

This film is for
Maggie, Amy and Holly
. . . and now,
Harry

Filmed at Cinecitta Studios SpA (Rome)
Pinewood Studios, England
and on Location in Italy and Spain

Copyright © Columbia Pictures Industries, Inc.
All Rights Reserved. MCMLXXXVIII

MPAA Rating: PG                    Running Time: 126 min.

## ACKNOWLEDGMENTS

For their unfailing cooperation and generous good humor through-out the compilation of the screenplay, the Publishers wish to thank Lester Borden, Rhonda Bryant, Mary Flanagan and Susan Pile of Columbia Pictures, Steve Abbott and Anne James of Prominent Features, and David Steinberg of Rollins, Morra & Brezner. For his extraordinary initiative and editorial wisdom, Mark Sterling Mixson deserves all our thanks and then some.

# THE ADVENTURES OF BARON MUNCHAUSEN
## The Novel

## by Terry Gilliam and Charles McKeown
with color and black-and-white illustrations

---

Baron Munchausen, one of the most famous liars in history, first recounted his adventures over two hundred years ago and since then they have been retold and added to by storytellers around the world. To the delight of frivolous adults and serious children who have followed Alice through the looking-glass and Dorothy down the yellow brick road, another most extraordinary adventure beckons. If you can keep up with the Baron and his little companion, Sally, you will ride a cannon ball over the invading Turks, sail to the moon in a hot-air balloon, plunge into the bowels of an erupting Mt. Etna, and join the South Pacific Fleet in the belly of a great sea monster.

**Fiction/Movies**
**ISBN: 1-55783-39-8**
**256 pages, 6 x 9**

The Baron's beleaguered city heaves with famine and devastation under the relentless attack of the Sultan's Turkish army. The Baron promises to end the siege and save the city, if only he can find his old comrades at arms: Albrecht, the strongest man on Earth; Berthold, the fastest man alive; Adolphus, who sees farther than a telescope; and Gustavus, who can blow harder than any hurricane.

The ladies of the town surrender their silken knickers to the Baron's seductive plan to weave a great hot-air balloon to carry him aloft in search of his friends. But the first comrade he meets is not old at all, but a young girl, Sally, who has stowed away on the Baron's makeshift craft.

At every port in their incredible voyage, the Baron finds time for romance and intrigue—and with each encounter, the Baron grows younger and stronger to meet the challenge of the savage Turks.

And as if fighting three-headed griffins and giant cyclopes weren't dangerous enough, the Baron is constantly dodging the spectre of Death, which shadows him throughout his journey.

Meanwhile, the city and its knickerless population withstand the continuous bombardments of the Turks in the hope that the Baron will return with his four remarkable comrades. Indeed, the Baron is reunited, despite unbelievable odds, with his comrades one by one, but reality remains insurmountable: each of his friends has grown old and weary. Albrecht falters, Berthold limps, Adolphus barely makes out the nose on his face, and Gustavus is coughing. Hardly the crew you'd enlist to save the day.

But appearances can be deceiving. The town is saved not by the outer strength of the Baron and his friends, but by inner strength and determined faith in the Baron and themselves. For a brief concentrated moment, their powers are focused and restored. The Sultan's army is trounced in a magical display of incredible, invincible strength.

The original ADVENTURES, written by Rudolf Erich Raspe in 1785, became an instant best-seller, and was hailed as a comic sensation in the satirical spirit of *Gulliver's Travels* and *Tom Jones*. The volume, illustrated by dozens of major artists in numerous editions, remained a constant companion of children around the world for nearly two centuries.

Terry Gilliam has now resurrected the Baron and his comrades in entirely new adventures capturing the Munchausen spirit in a volume destined to be a classic for generations to come. The new illustrations will keep the imagination soaring from the center of the earth to the moon.

# CURTAIN TIMES

**The New York Theater: 1965-1987**

## by Otis L. Guernsey, Jr.

Photographs by Martha Swope
Drawings by Al Hirschfeld

## —Critical Acclaim From *Playbill*—

"To see theater, and to see it whole—its hits and its flops, its creative talent and its business brains, its artistic achievements and its financial profiles, its oddities,

lapses, experiments and occasional world-resounding triumphs—one may read it all in the monumental new book CURTAIN TIMES by Otis L. Guernsey.

Season by season, CURTAIN TIMES covers two decades of Broadway and Off-Broadway theatrical life. However vociferously Guernsey's colleagues may disagree with a choice here or there, most would attest that he has never missed a worthy work.

The two-inch thick volume published by Applause Theatre Books is a compilation of his seasonal essays published in the *Best Plays* yearbooks (Dodd, Mead) which Guernsey has edited continuously since 1964. So in effect CURTAIN TIMES is 20 volumes in one, a bargain, a picture of New York theater as it has existed from 1965 to 1985, with a short summary bringing the volume right up to the present. The book has Martha Swope's photographs, Hirschfeld's drawings, and an index that makes it an invaluable reference work.

And not just theater is in its pages. Cultural shifts, social fashions and changes, underlying socio-political movements that inspire the life that appears on the stages are folded into Guernsey's season-by season accounts. The book incidentally includes informed comment on the passing journalistic scene with which Guernsey has a special familiarity.

In CURTAIN TIMES, Guernsey's special gift is to look for success on the stage instead of spending time deploring failure. He also takes a large and hopeful view of the future of New York theater while not ignoring its drawbacks and inherent weaknesses. Writing in the mid-sixties when new musicals were abundant and lived alongside many musical revivals, he calls attention to the need, never more urgent than today, for a place for the straight play. He writes:

'New York is a city where a very rich man may walk up a street with a very poor man and turn into their doors at homes which are side by side. The extreme condition of each points up the extreme condition of the other, by contrast, and this same relationship exists between the two genres of American stage works. Our musicals are richly displayed, year after year, in revival and in repertory, while our straight plays subsist mainly upon spare print on the library shelves; unfleshed.'

Theater encourages intense partisanship and tends to splinter off into narrow groups, often arousing strong critical passions. Guernsey, from where he sits, regards theatre differently—not dispassionately, to be sure, not without injecting his own point of view, but with more balance, less judgmentally, more as the historian who looks at the theater whole than the critic who finds its particular flaws. There are many critics, large and small, few custodians, few historians, so that Guernsey and his CURTAIN TIMES fill an especially valuable niche."

*"Otis L. Guernsey has leaped to the front of biographers of the American theatre. This is a uniquely comprehensive, uniquely detailed, and uniquely contemporaneous history of the New York theater. If there was only one book on contemporary theatre you could keep on your shelves, CURTAIN TIMES would have to be it.*
—Stages

*"What an excellent idea! CURTAIN TIMES puts in easy reach a trove of facts and figures nowhere else available documenting twenty-plus years of New York theater. This is an invaluable resource."*
—Hal Prince

**Theatre History/
New York/Reference
ISBN:
(paper) 0-936839-23-6
(cloth) 0-936839-24-4
620 pages, 6 x 9**

*"CURTAIN TIMES constitutes a veritable encyclopedia of theatrical criticism including charts, tables, photographs, and even drawings by the inimitable Hirschfeld, of the New York theater, 1965-1987. For anyone tuned into theatrical activity in New York in the decades since 1965, from the catastrophic rise in ticket prices to the catastrophic demise of theater landmarks, this volume is a must."*
—Choice

# A FISH CALLED WANDA

## The Screenplay

# by John Cleese

### Original Story by John Cleese and Charles Crichton

It comes as a great wave of relief to Python devotees everywhere that when Pythons Cleese and Palin gang up in this gangster *cum* romance *cum* as you please (leave at your own risk) movie event, that this mature work produced after nearly twenty years of colla-

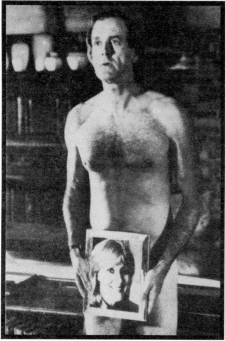

borative soul-searching, redefining of artistic goals, purging of existential ghouls, examination for social relevance and relentless self-censorship, ultimately results in what we had hoped for all along: their most immature movie ever. Of course, middle-age alone does not instant-immaturity confer. The Python arm reached out to seventy-eight-year-old director Charles Crichton to enforce a strict code of inane behavior. "Without the immaturity code," proclaims Crichton, "nothing but the most profound menopausal cinematic values would prevail."

Crichton should know. Many of his early films at Ealing studios, including the classic Lavender Hill Mob, became models for the whole Ealing comedy cult. "Discipline is what we learned at Ealing," barks Crichton, who holds Wanda's directorial rod to the sober antics of Kevin Kline, Jamie Lee Curtis and Maria Aitken. "I'm afraid I had to be quite severe with Cleese on several occasions." A FISH CALLED WANDA is at least for now the absolute uncappable cap to the careening careers of these madcapping farceurs.

BOOKSELLERS: Don't forget the fish market for WANDA. Every fishmonger in America will want a dozen.

Film/Screenplay
ISBN: 1-55783-033-9
112 pages, 5¹/₄ x 7³/₄
16 black and white stills

*"Wanda defies gravity, in both senses of the word, and redefines a great comic tradition."*
—Richard Schickel, *Time*

*"Like the cold slap of an English cod across the kisser...through sheer, manic resourcefulness manages not merely to fly, but to soar."*
—David Edelstein, *Village Voice*

# ACTING IN FILM
## The Applause Acting Series
## Based on the BBC Master Class Series
# by Michael Caine
## Edited by Maria Aitken

"You must always steal," writes Michael Caine, "but only from the best people. Steal any trick that looks worthwhile. If you see Vivien Leigh or Robert DeNiro or Meryl Streep do something stunningly effective, and you can analyze how he or she did it, then pinch it. Because," Caine explains, "you can be sure that they stole it in the first place." In ACTING IN FILM, Caine gives the reader a once-in-a-lifetime chance to rob him blind. The man who's hypnotized the camera lense for a quarter of a century exhibits the most closely guarded secrets to the art and science of spontaneity on screen, and then invites the reader to make them his own. Pearl by pearl, he lays out the Caine wisdom on everything from the screen test to set politics, voice, sound, and movement. He coaches the reader through script preparation, set decorum, working with the director, forming a character, and the film bureaucracy, and more. And for those who have higher aspirations, there's a chapter on "Being a Star."

MICHAEL CAINE

onACTING inFILM

Film/Acting
ISBN: 0-936839-86-4
96 pages, 5¹/2x 7³/4

BBC Videocassette
ISBN: 1-55783-034-7
(60 minutes)

Michael Caine dispels the mystical rites which surround film acting, and offers instead a practical philosophy of this minimalist art, told with straightforward clarity, wit and humor: "Don't sit as if you have nothing to say. You should be bursting with things to say. You just choose at this particular place and time, not to say them."

*"Witty, articulate and always entertaining, Michael Caine takes the nuts and bolts of film acting to pieces and gives away more trade secrets in the process than you thought existed."*
—*The London Sunday Times*

*"Caine demonstrates how sheer technique can mutate into something meaningful and moving."*
—*The London Observer*

*"Don't think of this as too esoteric or for actors only. You'll be laughing, absorbed and enchanted."*
—*London Daily Mail*

# UNFINISHED BUSINESS
## A Memoir : 1902-1988

# by John Houseman

U NFINISHED BUSINESS is an extraordinary memoir of a cultural hero, advancing bullishly into new artistic frontiers. We follow Houseman's corruscating path from The Mercury Theater, The Negro Theatre Project in Harlem, *Men from Mars*, *Citizen Kane*,

*Voice of America*, *The Blue Dahlia*, Brecht's *Galileo*, Playhouse 90, the American Shakespeare Festival, Juilliard, Paramount, Universal, MGM, the Acting Company, the Oscar, and beyond. After a lifetime (or five or six), John Houseman—his voice, his profile, his style—has been packaged as a household god, selling fast food and hard work out of every television set in America. Next to Cronkite, Houseman by the late seventies rated the highest credibility of any figure on television.

The *dramatis personae* of Houseman's chronicle represents an awesome roster of the arts in twentieth century America. When he isn't conspiring with Orson Welles, Virgil Thomson, Archibald McLeish or a dozen others to launch one of five major new theatre organizations, we find him in Hollywood with David O. Selznick, Alfred Hitchcock or Herman Mankiewicz producing one of his eighteen feature films. Far from simply being a great man at the right place at the right time, he has again and again made the place, staked out the territory, hoisted the revolutionary banner, and carried the movement past its inchoate stages. Just as we expect him to settle in, Houseman invariably moves on.

Media moguls, ideologues, lovers, wives, family, boards of directors, politicians all play their roles in one adventure-turned-institution to the next. Yet the subplot of this theatrical saga is unmistakably private, the ironic meditation on a life poised perpetually at the crossroads; the protagonist more often than not choosing a route blockaded by convention or fate. Houseman contemplates his own private demons, confronts them candidly with a mordant wit and a lively sense of despair as he enters the next cycle of a compelling journey. UNFINISHED BUSINESS reveals itself at turns as the unparalleled profile of a culture, and the incomparable autobiography of a man.

John Houseman's earlier books, *Run Through, Front and Center* and *Final Dress*, are among the most highly praised volumes of theatrical memoirs. In UNFINISHED BUSINESS, their 1500 pages have been distilled into a single volume with new revelations throughout and a major final chapter which for now brings the Houseman saga to a close.

*"...the truest chronicle of the American theatre...the best show in town."** —*Life*

*"One of the most brilliant volumes of theatrical reminiscence I've ever read."* —*New York Post*

*"Fascinating...I for one would be happy to follow his [life] for another thousand pages."* —Christopher Lehmann-Haupt
*The New York Times*

*"Such an entertaining book that it could be read, more or less shamefully, for the backstage gossip alone. But the fun and games are the least of it. 'Memoir' is too slight a word for this substantial, satisfyingly detailed, gracefully written account of an exciting period of American theatre."*
—Walter Kerr

**Autobiography/Theatre**
**ISBN: 1-55783-024-X**
**508 Pages, 5¹/₂ x 8¹/₄**

*"...a tense and brilliant performance, at opening-night pitch, with the theatrical virtues of pace, sharp lighting and perfect articulation...As the sardonic, personal history of a complicated man, it should interest even the unstagestruck. He makes us envious that we weren't around and young, exactly when he was."* —Walter Clemons
*Newsweek*

**\*Reviews of *Run Through, Front and Center* and *Final Dress*.**